THANKS FOR THE YELLOW ROSES

Jim Young

To Bill,

with everlasting gratitude for all you mean to me!

Love & hugs,

Jim Young

THANKS FOR THE YELLOW ROSES

ISBN: 9798737973773

Imprint: Independently published.

Copyright © 2021 by Jim Young. All rights reserved. No part of this book (in printed form, digitally, or any other form) may be used or reproduced in any manner whatsoever without written permission of the author. For information, contact:

Jim Young
creationspirit@gmail.com

ACKNOWLEDGEMENTS

These short stories tell of actual incidents along my life's journey. The stories are factually correct, yet occasionally names and places have been given alternative identities to protect the innocent and to render any political judgments powerless.

In every case, I am immensely grateful to the people, places and actual happenings for gracing my life beyond measure. Indeed, if I have learned nothing else in this lifetime, I have definitely come to understand that it is grace that truly guides and blesses our lives. And that our only real purpose is to stay aware of the still, small voice found only inward, that serves us this way…and then to demonstrate such adoration into completion.

Truly, I wish this for your life, as it has guided my own.

Jim Young

TABLE OF CONTENTS

Why Didn't God Take Me?

Beautiful, Very Beautiful

No More Inaugurals for Me

We Have Met the Enemy

Thanks for the Yellow Roses

The Jewel in the Lotus

The Truth That Quickens

How Could I?

You're Mayor of What?

Life's Just Funny That Way

    Stage One

    Stage Two

    Stage Three

    Stage Four

    Stage Five

Finis for Sure

On Pigeons and Other Important Matters

Surrender

WHY DIDN'T GOD TAKE ME?

It's a cloudless, blue-skied morning in Northern New Mexico. I wind my way through the hills on the "High Road" to Taos, my camera ready on the seat beside me. I begin the day wanting only to be open to the gift of the people I am on my way to photograph. They live in a tiny, predominantly Hispanic village called Truchas—Truchas meaning trout in Spanish—couched atop a plateau at the foot of the Truchas peaks in the Sangre de Cristo (Blood of Christ) Mountain Range. One of the peaks reports a large cross on its crest, seeming to protect the inhabitants of this quaint village from harm. Nature's setting calls forth feelings of welcome.

Its endearing features are the aging adobe homes, unpaved streets, and its people: the warm and generous elderly and those they raise in semi-poverty, and now, yet another, younger generation. The village is sprinkled with art galleries, bed and breakfast inns, its own general store and a gasoline pump or two. Until now, Truchas has perhaps been best known by outsiders as the setting for the 1980's Robert Redford movie, *Milagro Beanfield War*, and for its lone restaurant, The Truchas Mountain Cafe, written about in the New York Times years ago as *the* place to warm your belly with authentic Mexican food. The remnants of movie sets are a lingering reminder of exciting times for the few who remain from that scene. The divorced proprietors of the café, for example, have gone their separate ways, passing their former haven through the hands of local realtors on to yet another gallery for local artists. And life goes on in Truchas.

I shift into second gear so I can make the grade past the first of several outposts of local artisans' wares. I take note of the cemetery filled with brightly colored plastic flowers, embraced by the azure blue skies and the craggy peaks sprinkled with freshly dropped snow. Suddenly, my instincts lead me to apply the brakes so I can view a particularly unusual gravesite more closely. The site is adorned with two wrought iron renditions of motorcycles straddling a straw covered mound. Having often wondered what prompted this unusual form of burial, something within moves me to create several images I can use for later reflection. Moved by this episode, I forge my way up the hill yet further, catching the vast expanse stretching out behind me in my rear view mirror.

Soon, I come upon the landmarks that welcome

visitors to the village. Mostly they are signs of times past: a dilapidated barn, groaning as it leans on one side, much like the hillside upon which it rests; a year-round Christmas Star perches precariously on the edge of its leaky roof. Next to the barn is a sight familiar to most travelers of this route: a large, aging, wooden cross, outlined by Christmas lights, jutting into the sky like a Ponderosa pine announcing its rightful place in the world. My heart mellows at the sight, softened even further by the memories of having looked after a gallery in town with my former spouse at Christmas time some seven years earlier.

In my peripheral vision, I sense the intrusion of the more modern-day glistening, metallic pole, with *Truchas, NM* glaring from the cold, green state highway sign riveted on top, and my heart goes into a lurch. I stop the car and exit to view this contrasting juxtaposition of the past and present from my knees, recording the unsettling composition somewhat in dismay.

My appointment is for nine o'clock. It had come about rather circuitously. Earlier in the summer, on a plane over the Atlantic on the way to Greece, I felt prompted to take on the project of photographing elderly women in villages, both on the islands I would be visiting, and on the mainland where my late father's surviving family still lives. The working title, *WOMEN OF THE VILLAGE*, came to me and guided me on my way. It had been a rather profound coming to that point, for all at once I felt tugging within me compassion and love for the elderly women who at one time were the center of their immediate and extended families, but who now seemed to be all but forgotten. Such women, their hearts filled with love, faces creased with wisdom, and eyes filled with dignity, have a presence of such elegance as to open the hearts and souls of all who notice. "I'll do my part to see that they are remembered," I heard my inner self proclaim.

Just as vividly, on the return trip home to Santa Fe I recall my original vision taking new shape. I felt the necessity to extend my heartfelt search to include elderly women of villages in my own region of New Mexico, and then on to other regions of the United States, and even other countries. For one who sees with the heart, life's staples of elegance and dignity can be found everywhere. I mentioned the idea to my tax accountant at the time, and she suggested I visit some elderly friends of hers in Truchas, where she also lives. So I began by arranging this appointment to photograph several elderly Hispanic women, followed with an inner commitment to photograph others as they come into my journey.

Still displeased by the double message from the symbolic signposts at the entry to the village, but somewhat more detached than earlier, I search for the designated location noted on my hand-scribbled scrap of note paper. After a slightly confused attempt to locate the residence, it suddenly becomes clear to me that this is the place: a large, gray, stucco rectangle planted catty-corner to the restored church now used only infrequently by the local Penitentes. Not knowing quite what to expect, I gather my equipment and somewhat tentatively ring the doorbell. I peer through the lace curtains, letting the voices inside tempt an analysis of who might greet me.

The door opens slowly, and this beaming face of a woman greets me as if a long-lost friend has just graced her threshold. "Good morning, come in, come in. I'm Susie, come in." I introduce myself and ease into the warmth of what seems like a combination living room, bedroom. Suddenly I am consumed by the smells and sounds of a country breakfast being prepared in the small, boxy kitchen, barely large enough to contain a wood-stove, oversized refrigerator, sink, small aging wooden kitchen table, and a tiny wash-stand with water, soap and towel ready to greet the next user. "Come in," implores Suzie, "we're just having breakfast, we hope we won't hold you up. Would you like a tortilla? I'm just making them fresh."

"Just a cup of coffee would be fine, thank you," I respond, stepping further into the toasty kitchen to meet Susie's daughter, Kathy, and Kathy's husband, John, along with two young boys, actually the couple's grandchildren, Daryll, 5, and Andrew, age 4. They're all in various stages of breakfast. Kathy and John appear too young to be grandparents. We exchange greetings and before I retreat into the living room to sip on the freshly brewed coffee, I watch intently as Susie kneads a tortilla, lovingly embracing it between her palms. It's clear that the tortilla hugs her back.

While I sip coffee in the comfort of the sparsely furnished room, I am bathed in the early morning light that drifts in through the lacey yellow curtains adorning the entry door, spreading a buttery cast on the wall beyond. Two miniature pueblo-style wooden ladders of the type sold to tourists guard the entry corner. Several straight-back chairs with cushions of varying sizes and shapes line the buttery wall like wooden toy soldiers. Two double beds jutting out from the opposite wall brace a scattering of plants in between, and pictures of Jesus and family members filling the wall greet the knowing eye. A few ristras, strings of dried red chili peppers, frame a quote about mothers: "A Rose is as Tender as a Mother's Heart." Any doubt I may have had about this being the place to be vanishes.

Suzie anxiously tells me several times that she doesn't want to waste my time and informs me that she needs to call her sister, Fede, so she can join us from her home nearby. Before making the call, Susie introduces me to her 93 year-old mother, Leonardita. "I still have to brush out her hair," proclaims Susie, "and we'll have to get her out of her housecoat for the picture," she issues. "Don't make any fuss, Susie, I want only to create images as they show up naturally," I respond. She pays absolutely no attention to me and goes about her way. I smile inwardly.

As she heads toward the phone to summon her sister, Susie brings me two rather worn journals and a well-read copy of a newspaper about times past. Proudly, she points to the articles about her mother, and another about how she and her mother had been included in the movie, *The Milagro Beanfield War*, utilizing their cozy kitchen. I read them with great interest as she makes her telephone call.

When she returns from the conversation with her sister, Susie asks me in rapid-fire fashion about my background, where I live, and what brought me to Truchas. Her interest peaks when I tell her that my former wife and I had tended a gallery just up the street a few years ago. Then, when I indicate that we had looked at property there as a possible location for our home, she immediately becomes helpful by offering information about eight acres for sale just up the road, at about $20,000 per acre. "But you could sell off two-thirds of it, if you think that's too expensive, you know." We talk about the sad condition of rising taxes and other costs elevated by outsiders purchasing property and starting galleries and such in the community. "They say that new galleries will make us famous again, make it good, but most of us just can't keep up with higher taxes and costs," she deplores. I am delighted when she spices up our running conversation with a *pero* and *bueno* now and then.

Susie's sister, Fede, arrives. There is an unmistakable family resemblance, which shows itself in looks, patterns of speech and body language. At one point when we are alone in our conversation, Fede gets up from her chair and fetches a photocopy of a picture. It is of her granddaughter, alongside her motorcycle. She haltingly tells me of how her granddaughter had been killed riding it, just two and a half months ago. Slowly, Fede returns the picture to its place, on the bed just beneath the portrait of Jesus, and tears paint a portrait of her sadness. In that instant, I know why I had been drawn to the gravesite guarded by motorcycles. And I join Fede on her canvas of life.

By now, the two young children have grown curious, and begin to show interest in this stranger in their midst. They both have freshly cut, close-cropped hair. They approach daringly and gleefully take to my rubbing the stubble on their heads. I tease them some about their age and Andrew asks me how old I am. After I respond with a playful "87," Andrew races to the kitchen to ask his grandfather how old he is. I hear his amused response, delivered with a chuckle, "Well, I'm 88!" Meanwhile, Daryll shows me his booklet of 152 self-adhesive animal stickers and eventually places a parrot delicately on my shoulder, as well as his own. We playfully *squawk* at one another.

Fede repeats the fact that there are four generations represented in the house that morning: her mother, she and her sister, her daughter and husband, and their two grandchildren. "Their mother is in Colorado, or we'd have five generations here," she instructs. "My father's in jail, you know," Daryll innocently informs me. I am rather startled by his frank admission, but make nothing of it by dismissing it with a simple, non-judgmental, "Oh, that's interesting."

I ease into photographing by framing a portrait of Leonardita and, bit by bit, include others until each of the four generations has been added to the family bouquet. Chatter abounds, the children come and go, and directions come from daughters and other family members to great-great grandmother to help her keep focused. Leonardita shows her humble attitude by rarely looking directly into the camera. But others want the usual "say Jesus" pose the children comically display when it comes their turn.

Somewhat surprised by the large amount of film I am using, I back off for a bit to see what might better come next. I choose to photograph in natural light only, so I am careful in my discernment. I decide to shift my location to the other side of the room and open the front door to let in more of that warm, morning sun, and it turns out to be a good decision.

At this point I limit the photos to Susie, Fede, their mother and the boys. Leonardita springs to life and hugs the boys as they squirm to get in her lap, eager to be closer to her. First one, and then the other, wiggles to her embrace, and the group takes on a special radiance. I retreat to my wide-angle lens and record the grandparent's glee over what they are witnessing by reflecting them in the mirror on the wardrobe nearby.

That about wraps it up for the morning. Things seem to be complete, so I begin packing my equipment. I am feeling privileged to have been taken into the life of this wonderfully warm and generous family. My attention shifts dramatically when Andrew and Daryll begin to lay barrages of hugs and kisses on Leonardita. I quickly pull out my camera, load it, and let the bliss of the moment be captured on the film. Much of what I am taking in through the viewfinder is also etching a permanent image on the lining of my heart.

After repacking, I am gifted by hugs from the entire family and feel filled with blessings. Susie and Fede invite me to return in December to photograph them making holiday cookies. As I already had promised them that I would return with some prints, this is a welcome invitation. I immediately accept.

As I wind my way back toward home, I find myself in the warm glow I felt all throughout the morning. The thought occurs to me that in my own family I am missing the love, caring and nurturing found in close family relationships like the one I have just witnessed. Right then and there I vow to rekindle that flame.

On the way down the hill toward Chimayo, I am strangely prompted to look for my reading glasses, and make a thorough search of my pockets and the front seat, but to no avail. I bring the car to a stop, and look through my camera gear. Not finding the glasses, I reverse my route to re-engage my new friends. I ring the doorbell, turning the knob with ease. This time there is no chatting behind the entry and the door opens quickly. There stands Susie with her usual broad smile, proclaiming knowingly, "You're just like me, some days I don't even know where my head is." She beckons me to enter and goes to the kitchen, and I trail behind. She plucks my battered glass case off the stove and drops it into my expectant hand amidst my immediate expression of gratitude.

Fede is washing dishes and points with pride to

the array of family photos thumbtacked along both sides of the door jamb. "Look at all those grandchildren and great-grandchildren," exclaims Susie, taking over for the more reluctant Fede. "You know, we've lost only one 26 year-old girl and one 27 year-old boy out of all those children," she informs me as I am led out of the kitchen. "And do you know what my mother said when we lost them?" she asks. "She said, 'Why didn't God take me instead of them? I've had a long and good life.' Can you image her?" And the whole morning once again comes sharply into focus.

As we head out of the kitchen, I notice a Christmas cactus ready to bloom, and tell them how much I love ours. "Oh, that's Maria," said Susie. "Maria?" I ask. "Yes, that's Aunt Maria to me. She always had a beautiful Christmas cactus in the house, and this reminds me of her, so I call it Maria."

Not wanting to be left out, Fede joins in escorting me out to my car. She offers to have me stop at the Dunkin' Donuts so one of their grandchildren who works there can treat me on the way home. I gratefully decline and thank them again for their generous hospitality. Susie walks beside the car, guiding me from my parking spot, out between her house and the neighbor's. She then carefully leads me to the main street that bisects this quaint village. I roll down the passenger window and bid Susie a final, "*Hasta luego*," and she, in turn, delivers a gleeful, "*Hasta pronto*," on the end of her waving arm.

As I edge toward home, I suddenly realize that what had earlier seemed like incongruous welcome signs at the edge of town are no longer troubling me.

And a deep sigh takes me to a state of inner knowing as I pass the brace of motorcycles in the cemetery down below.

BEAUTIFUL, VERY BEAUTIFUL

Her name is Maria. From the poetic soul of a smile she gives me as she waves in the midst of watering her plants, I have a sense she is a Maria even before she tells me her name.

Because I speak only enough Greek to be a "dangerous American," I ask, using the only means I know how, if I may create her photograph. I gesture with my camera cradled in one hand, saying, "pahrahkahló," please. Gracefully, she nods her consent and straightens out her plants instead of her clothes, brushing back her long string of curly hair that has been freed from her bobby pin by the tasks at hand. She transforms completely into the most elegant of women, regal-like in her demeanor and stance. She tosses her head to one side, and a warm Mona Lisa-like smile caresses my film as her side-lit misty skin glistens like the moon's reflections on a dew-filled night.

In an instant, she motions me to come. "Éleh! éleh!" Come, come, she suggests. I beckon my spouse, Helen Jane, who is studying the sensuously structured abandoned church next door and she joins me to greet Maria.

This was about the halfway point of our trip to Greece. It had begun nearly three weeks ago in Athens, where we visited our cousin Tasos and his 90-year old mother, Aunt Artemis, who speaks not one word of English. Neither Helen Jane nor I speak much Greek, but we got along famously with Aunt Artemis in Athens those eight days. Each day we were bathed in her affectionate energy and blessed by her love-filled food. The central female character in *Like Water for Chocolate*, the Mexican movie about love's impact on cooking, had nothing on Aunt Artemis. No, indeed.

Somehow we managed to communicate, even if, on one occasion, I got playfully slapped on the side the head when I misunderstood Aunt Artemis' request to get something from the cupboard, I know not what. I mistakenly ventured to the refrigerator, instead. "Jeemy, Jeemy!" was her playful response, hand waving in protest over my lack of language skills, finally striking me a playful, glancing blow just hard enough to burp a laugh from the middle of my dodging antic. It was even funnier when we returned several weeks later to Aunt Artemis' apartment, having learned a half-dozen new words at most. At dinner one evening she told

Tasos how happy she was that "Jeemy" had progressed so well in learning Greek. Love covers a host of sins.

We followed our stay in Athens with eight days on the island of Mytilini, or Lesbos, as we Americans call it, one of Greece's largest islands just off the coast of Turkey. Tasos wanted to show us his favorite island. It turned out to be a paradise, both photographically and in all ways imaginable.

Earlier, while flying over the Atlantic on the way to Greece, I had declared my intention to begin a new photo essay, *WOMEN OF THE VILLAGE*. I would thus pay homage to the elderly village women who are the foundation of their families worldwide. And now, on the near-deserted streets of villages throughout the island, time and time again I meet women in their 70's, 80's and 90's. I approach them in my hopeful attempts to create a lasting image of the elegance, the endless dignity and unfathomable depth of their souls. Each time, I hold my camera in one hand, extending the other with a voice pleading, "Pahrahkahló," please.

Often the response comes either as a look of disbelief that I have asked this person, of all people, to create a photo with me, or as a look that indicates a clear lack of understanding of what I am asking. If the latter is the case, I simply ask again, making it even more obvious that I want only to create their image, gesturing even more dramatically with the camera. Usually they pause and ponder the request. As they do, I merely convey—by saying "oréhoss," beautiful—what I believe to be true: the eyes are the windows of the soul, and the personification of beauty. Most seem quite astonished to be called beautiful, some making it obvious that they think I am only flattering them.

But when I have their attention, I move closer, gently and slowly, so as not to frighten them, and point with my index and middle fingers to their eyes, saying "Oréhoss, polee oréhoss," beautiful, very beautiful. On every occasion, this simple clarification, that I see the beauty of their soul, makes them completely receptive to our co-creation. When the exchange of creative energy is completed, most thank me profusely before I have a chance to let the words of gratitude escape from my own mouth, wanting me think it is they who are honored. I hasten to make it clear that I, too, am honored—and profoundly grateful. And authentic relationship is either created, or renewed, depending on one's perspective.

Examples abound of images feminine in nature. A cat screwing its neck to watch two women

weaving both fabric and words into life's stories;
a grandmother framing her love for her
granddaughter in a lovely silhouette beneath the
shade of a grape-covered arbor; a ninety-
something-year-old woman, consumed in black

from head to toe, hunched over from an advanced stage of osteoporosis, sewing needle and thread in one hand, a loaf of fresh baked bread under the other arm, graciously welcoming my approach; all ages of women, mostly dressed in black, tending to family graves and monuments high on the hill overlooking the brilliantly sunlit bay on a late Saturday afternoon. Each of these, and scores more along the way, convince me that being summoned to this body of work is both powerful and necessary.

And, now the same on Skopelos, a charming, quaint fishing island just under two hours by hydrofoil off the mid-eastern, mainland shore. In many cases, "conversations" are of a different, deeper communication when both parties share, despite their respective language deficiencies. It feels like heart language, clear and deeply understood.

Helen Jane and I are now climbing three flights of stairs, following Maria—some twenty years older, but far more agile and less winded in her scaling ability than we are. We reach the top of the stairs and follow her through a private tour of her typically sparse surroundings. Sparse, yes, but her love is everywhere present in the colors which complement the brilliant whitewashed walls, the photos which greet us as if we are new members of her family, the placement of the simple furniture which bids a welcome. The three floors of tiny rooms are stacked one on top of another, connected by the poorly lighted, steep narrow wooden staircase. This is the simple life.

Maria gestures for us to sit down at the kitchen table, apparently asking if we'd like some water. Seeing that we don't understand, she reaches for a glass and points to the faucet, and we respond with a delighted, "Neh, neh," yes, yes. We all laugh at this humble beginning to our communication and together enjoy a cool glass of water as Maria "explains" that it has been very hot, so she had opened a large beach umbrella on the balcony that extends from the third story entry to the kitchen in order to create some badly needed shade. A cool breeze suddenly wafts across our gathering and a feeling of welcome permeates our hearts.

By gestures, and a sixth sense that somehow lets us know exactly what is being said, Maria invites us to lunch the next day, at one o'clock—or at least that's what we think she's saying to us. She mentions her grandson, Dimitrios (also my baptismal name) and his American girlfriend. We assume they'll be at lunch until Maria informs us that Chrissie is back in the States and won't be joining us. After a wondrous conversation, we bid Maria a fond farewell, promising to be there the next day, promptly at one o'clock.

As we awake the next day, Helen Jane declares her desire to cast her pastel paints upon the memory of a scene from the day before. I sense this is not only right for Helen Jane, but feel a special calling for myself. After a delightfully simple breakfast at our friendly hotel, the Agnanti, Helen Jane and I seal our pledge to creative solitude with a farewell kiss, and I depart. I wind my way up the narrow, slate-covered streets between crisp white buildings, dappled here and there with pots of bright flowers and simple, decorative doors interrupted most always with lace-curtained windows. The streets are clean and fresh, the product of daily sweeping and scrubbing by the woman of the house in each instance. I rest for a moment and am taken by the similarity between the azure blue sky here and my home in Santa Fe. The brilliant light and clear skies make everything amazingly clear for miles and miles. The only difference is the quality of the light: if possible, it is even a warmer hue here, more golden in character.

I create a photo here, another there, but of spaces, not people, the latter which is what I am really destined to do. I am just awaking my photographic sensibility. It is now about 10:30 in the morning. Just as I begin to think this will be a wasted morning (how many times this has happened on my life's journey!), I glance to the right, up a long, ascending walkway. It is lined mostly with whitewashed, two story homes painted with lush, brightly-colored hanging plants, the entries dotted here and there with familiar pots of geraniums. A fair distance beyond the intersection from which I observe this scene, I see two women, one middle-aged, and another much older, donned in the now familiar post-mortem black.

The younger of the two women is sweeping the area around her entry—that, too, a familiar sight. Simultaneously, she carries on a spirited conversation with the older woman. As I find out later, I mistakenly took the older woman to be the younger woman's mother. So much for quick judgments. I edge closer, creating a few images of this relationship before either of them notices me and become self-conscious. The younger woman finally notices my behavior and bids me a good-morning, "Kahleeméhrah, kahleeméhrah."

"Kahleeméhrah," I return with a smile and we are instant companions. I sit on one of the wide, shallow steps to catch my breath and she asks, in Greek, if I'd like some water. I understand well enough this time, and respond with gratitude, "Neh, ehfkhahreesto'," yes, thank you. She calls inside to yet another Maria, suggesting something I don't understand. We converse by sign language for a few minutes until I see the younger woman becoming impatient over the delay of her request being fulfilled. She sticks her head into the entry and calls to Maria once again. I echo her, "Maria, Maria," which delights both women. Momentarily Maria, a late teenager, emerges with a smile on her face carrying several glasses of water and a bounty of cognac on a circular tray. "Hi," she says, "I'm Maria, and you are?," in perfect English. I'm Jim, actually I was baptized Dimitrios," I convey in response. I explain my heritage, which she conveys to all present, and suddenly I feel a gentle, warming shift in our relationship take place.

The next half hour is invested with openness shared normally only by long-time friends. We had become that it seems. It turns out that Maria is 18 years old, and a political science student at a university in Thessaloniki, northern Greece. She asks my background and communicates it to her mother and the older woman, who turns out to be a neighbor and close friend of the family. I ask permission and, gaining it, create several more images of the triad, plus the recent newcomers to the array from the two-story home just up the street. Then there is the man of the house hanging over the gateway entry and his wife cheerfully participating from amidst the thick growth of hanging plants.

The elderly neighbor asks Maria something and in turn, Maria asks where home is for me. "United States," I respond, and Maria repeats to the elder, "Amerikani." "Amerikani," the woman says, and proceeds to tell Maria a brief story that sends Maria and her mother into a fit of laughter. When she regains her composure, Maria shares the story with me. "She says her last husband was an American, but he's dead now." As Maria says the words, dead now, her neighbor repeatedly throws both arms crosswise across her bosom, imitating her late husband lying dead, saying "dead" with gesticular language several times. She mimics like a female Charlie Chaplin and I show my amusement without constraint. Maria continues, "She also says that she would

be pleased if you could find her another
American for a husband, but he must be old and

ready to die in only a few weeks." Doubling over
with laughter, I almost knock over the remaining

cognac and water, and the entire gathering shows its appreciation of my appreciation by joining me in chorus-like fashion. At that, I ask if I may take a portrait of the jester and she obliges in full display of her dignity—with a good portion of humor in her eyes. My father would have labeled her eyes "mischievous," and he would have been absolutely correct in this case. I notice that it's time for me to leave, so Helen Jane and I won't be late for our one o'clock engagement. After I obtain their address so I can send them a copy of the photos, I descend the way I came, turning to wave a fond good-bye, still tickled by my pledge to find my new friend another—albeit a guaranteed short-lived—American husband.

Helen Jane and I arrive at Maria's just as the clock strikes one. We rap on the front door, but Maria apparently doesn't hear us. So I beckon her from the first floor entry to the third floor balcony overhead, singing her name liltingly, "Maria—Maria—Maria." Her beaming face greets us over the railing above, "Éleh, éleh." So we truck the upward journey once again and are greeted by joyous hugs and the blissful aromas of a loving Greek kitchen as we cross the threshold into the crisp, cool blue and white room. Despite the breeze flowing from one side of the house to the other, Maria is glistening from the preparations she is concocting for her guests.

She promptly introduces us to her grandson and we strike up the "grand inquisition," first making it clear to Dimitrios that we *think* we have been invited to their house for lunch. Dimitrios smiles, saying, "Oh, that's probably right. My grandmother invites everyone in for lunch. She told me about having had her picture taken, and how she enjoyed it," he reports. Later, when I offer to create an image of him with Maria, he gracefully declines, making it clear he has little need for such things.

We dine primarily on boiled squid, a tasty delicacy bathed simply in olive oil, garlic, and lemon. Helen Jane declines for the most part, but I delight in what is a new dish for me. Delight, delight and delight even more. In a flash, a man we readily recognize from the pier below storms into the kitchen, hugging his mother and son, speaking half in Greek and half in English. Stavros is Maria's son, and is "responsible" for filling sixty hotel rooms a night during the high season. He proudly puffs out his chest, declaring, "I'm the best on the pier, and everybody knows it!" And we believe him, despite the hint of disdain his son shows for this display. I find him bold, yet charming in his own way.

In the middle of luncheon "conversation," in which it is quite apparent that Maria is not too happy with her son, we hear a ship's horn announcing its immanent arrival at the pier. Stavros drops his fork like a hot coal, pulls his short-sleeved shirt back on over his sleeveless undershirt, quickly hugs his mother, and blurts a good-bye to the rest of us. He is gone as quickly and directly as he entered. "That's my dad," sighs Dimitrios, and we continue our meal in the midst of the space that pronouncement creates. For the rest of our stay on Skopelos, we occasionally watch Stavros on the pier with care and find that he does indeed know the truth about himself. He is the best at what he does.

It is the next day. While on the bus returning from a relaxing day at the beach, I realize that I must have left my cap at Maria's the day before. I suggest to Helen Jane that she return to the hotel while I find out if my hat is at Maria's. She agrees, I suspect, eager to continue the newfound pattern of taking a siesta before dinner, and we head our different ways for the time being. I walk along the harbor's edge, taking in sights and smells from the tavernas that line the walkway, admiring the simplicity of the Greek lifestyle and the sensuality of their food. After climbing what seem like all the stairs on the island, first past a beautiful orthodox church and then remnants of several churches and houses, I rest near the top of my destination, letting the late afternoon golden sun permeate my every cell. I feel very fortunate to be in my father's country again, and my roots are refreshed by fond memories of him.

After a few moments in this eternity, I turn to locate Maria's house and expectantly knock on the front door. Again, her beaming face welcomes me like an ocean bird floating over the edge of the railing greeting the fishing vessels at the end of the day. And again we negotiate understanding with gestures and laughs. In a moment, I am in her kitchen asking if she has found my cap, but alas, she hasn't seen it. She invites me to join her for a cup of Greek coffee, kaféh, and I gladly accept. We "chat" about this and that and as I finish my coffee I ask Maria if she would "read" my cup, a famous custom in older Greek homes. She is delighted at my request and tells me of my good fortune, showing me the symbols etched on the inside of the cup wall that make it so. She then quite astonishingly points to a large heart-shaped symbol on the opposite side and tells me I am connected to a big heart, meaning God, and looks up to heaven, placing her hand reverently on her heart, as though to acknowledge God's presence in our midst. There is more, and we exchange words of common understanding and affirmation. Warmth abounds.

Quickly, and quite unexpectedly, the smile fades from Maria's face. She stops and becomes very melancholy, lapsing into her own space, diving into a world of her own. After a fashion, she snaps back to the present and proceeds to tell me of her contrasting relationships with her son and grandson, saddened by the discontent over her feelings about her son, yet tearfully joyful at the thoughtfulness of her grandson. She weeps unabashedly, convulsing in the pain of thought. I hold her hand in compassionate understanding, and her sweaty trembling begins to subside. Time stands still in relationship. I know in that instant, as I have felt many times before, that heart language transcends all cultures. All one needs to do for others is to be fully present to them in relationship; a lesson for the ages. And I am grateful for this reminder of the treasure it is.

Maria brings herself back to everyday life and makes sure I understand that she wants Helen

Jane and me to return the next day at midmorning for coffee. Hers is the best, she assures me, and I agree—both with her assessment of her brew-making ability and with her generous invitation to return with Helen Jane the next day. I kiss her hand as we separate from a parting hug and tears glisten in her eyes once again. I join Maria on her canvas of life.

It is the next morning and I am filled with joy over having photographed several new creations, each time with similar results: an open invitation into the soul-space of the created. And a new friend has etched rich memories on my heart. Helen Jane is photographing scenes for potential pastel paintings when she returns home and occasionally our energies embrace one another in our separate, yet interdependent ways. She photographs me parting from a conversation with an elderly woman who has just co-created a portrait with me. As I kiss the women's hand in a gesture of thanks, I hear the click of Helen Jane's camera and I know we are all connected in the only way that really matters.

It is ten o'clock as we approach Maria's front door. As has become custom by now, we are greeted with hugs and penetrating smiles. Maria promptly serves us coffee, much stronger than that to which we Americans are accustomed. We "chat" as usual, and I ask Maria if she will read Helen Jane's cup. As she did with me, Maria swells with pride and her face brightens, while concentrating deeply on the grounds that paint a personal landscape on the bottom and sides of the cup. She reports a few things, this time with seemingly little impact, until she proclaims with a broad smile, "Aurea, polee aurea." As Helen Jane is expressing her appreciation, an elderly woman enters the kitchen, apparently a close friend of Maria's. They embrace and Maria immediately becomes more animated as they separate. We are introduced. "This is Eleni," Maria gestures, and Eleni (Helen in Greek) greets us with ease.

She sits down between Helen Jane and me as Maria offers her coffee. Eleni declines and asks for water instead. Eleni notices my camera and exchanges a few words with Maria. I immediately suggest that I create a group picture of the women. Maria protests only moderately. Helen Jane does not like her picture taken at all, but is a good sport and agrees to go along for the ride. Eleni begins to decline, saying she is not dressed up enough to be photographed. I am amused at her self-description, because she is dressed to the nines, as the expression goes, but she plays it to the hilt and she and Maria chatter as Maria takes her to her bedroom. Helen Jane is obviously as amused by Eleni's attitude as I am. A few minutes later, they reemerge with Eleni's hair combed differently and wearing one of Maria's summer shawls draped elegantly over her shoulders. Maria hasn't changed a thing. She only brushes a few loose strands of hair away from her face and they join Helen Jane on the banco-like seating behind the kitchen table.

All at once the three get very somber, which doesn't fit their group character at all. Fear and reluctance prevail. Just a few minutes ago they were chatting like old friends at a party and laughing at whatever amused them at the moment. I make a strange screeching sound just to break the ice and Maria and Eleni break up uncontrollably. Just as quickly as the ice is broken they put on their invisible shields of frost once again. Now I discern that Eleni is protesting that she is too fat to photograph, mimicking her girth by blowing out her cheeks like a musician playing a saxophone. I respond by turning my face into the opposite, imitating a fish's mouth with sunken cheeks and Eleni loses control of herself; Maria is thoroughly amused at

Eleni's reaction and Helen Jane is laughing uproariously at the two of them.

I snap a few photos, rearrange a few things on the table to make it less cluttered, and create the fish face again. Again Eleni and Maria lose control and Helen Jane sits in amusement over the entire scene. We have a grand time of it all, but Helen Jane and I sense it is time for us to leave. We spread kisses and hugs all around as we depart.

When we arrive at the bottom of the stairs and emerge onto the sidewalk beneath the balcony, we find Maria and Eleni waving to us as they laughingly try to imitate the fish face. I return the favor and Helen Jane and I depart walking hand in hand, reminded once again that life is its own reward.

As we approach the pier alongside our favorite restaurant, we come across Dimitrios basking in the sun, musing privately about one thing or another. We greet him and describe our morning with Maria and Eleni, and Helen Jane tells him of having her cup read. Dimitrios laughs, and says "I'll bet she told you your cup was polee aurea, didn't she?"

Helen Jane looks baffled and Dimitrios clarifies, "Well, that's how she makes friends, after all. You wouldn't want to deprive her of that would you?"

NO MORE INAUGURALS FOR ME

I want to tell you a few stories about my Mom and Dad. They didn't actually die. They just traded in their earthly asbestos suits for sets of angel wings. In any event, both my Dad and Mom have passed into the new realm, flew the coup, returned to their full-time Spirit Beingship, whatever terminology makes you aware of your immortality instead of believing in the fictitious mortality concept that has been foisted upon us. To the mortal way of thinking, there is birth and death, but, in reality, life simply and beautifully and faithfully goes on and on and on in various forms.

I have come to believe that stories are one of the main reasons we come to this planet: for us to actually become the stories that will inform and inspire others to become what we all really are, lovers of the first order. Our stories can inspire and inform. It's our stories that embolden, that ennoble, that dignify one another. Our stories are what transform fear into being love—as the only reality that is. It's what gives life its purpose. We all have purpose, and I don't mean purpose in the sense of different strokes for different folks. I mean we all have just one purpose, one in the same for each of us, only we demonstrate it differently among us, using our innate gifts each in our own way. This is where my stories about Mom and Dad begin to take focus.

Dad was a painter—primarily a house painter, but also a painter of buildings, bridges, and the like. In the latter years of his life (he passed at 78 while still working full-time), he mostly painted houses. He lovingly turned them into homes. I have always admiringly referred to him as the Leonardo da Vinci of house painting, because he was an artist first and foremost, above all. The houses he painted were rendered with the utmost care and attention. Indeed, they became pieces of art.

But this was not where his artistry stopped, not by a long shot. He painted life with his stories, his funny sayings, his insistence on asking every housewife who kept an eye on him while he painted if they had something cold to drink. Inevitably they would bring him some water. And just as inevitably he would say in a laughing voice, "What, no orange juice, no pineapple juice, no cranberry juice? Ah, this country no good, Chicago all right!" Now just try to continue a conversation with that as an opener!

Of course, it was just a statement of his humor. And it never seemed to matter if anyone else laughed or not. It was good enough for him that he enjoyed doing it.

From time to time Dad was also a restaurant owner. And he loved to tell stories. As a Greek immigrant, his naturalized citizen's semi-thick Greek accent made his stories even more interesting. Some of my friends used to smile at Dad's accent. I just thought it was normal for him, and enjoyed how he said things in ways we wouldn't. Like saying sheep for ship, and mischeevous for mischievous. The long and short of it is that he brought life into the ways he communicated with people. He uplifted them with his compassion, emboldened them with his integrity, enlivened them with his sense of humor, lit them up with his extraordinary respect for human dignity.

He didn't talk about these things. He lived them. That is the real point of it all—the point of life, that is. That was his purpose: to live as the loving being he was, true to himself, with his delightful, loving personality showing through, no matter what it was he was doing. His story, and thus his purpose, was simply being the lover he was. Our purpose is exactly that. No more. No less.

I recall a bit of a story Dad told me one sunny afternoon in our home town of Silver Creek, NY, population 3200, counting everything that moved, including leaves on trees. Actually, it was more like a moral lesson. I was about ten years old, maybe 12, but no older. I liked helping my dad in the small restaurant he ran at the time. His partner, Dan, had died from cancer, and Dad had to run it by himself, with Mom, my sister Virginia and me helping as we could. Actually, Virginia was more interested in boys by then, so I don't recall her being around that much, but I could be mistaken. And our brother, Bill, was much too young to help. Dad worked very long hours and it nearly burned him out and did him in. As a matter of fact, good old Dr. Barresi once said to him, "Harry, you'd better stop smoking and drinking so much coffee or you'll be dead a lot sooner than you think." That one admonition from someone he respected was all Dad needed. Immediately he sold the restaurant and went back to painting for a living.

Anyhow, late one muggy afternoon in mid-July, just as the shade began to cool the sidewalk in front of the restaurant, I was sitting on one of the dozen or so stools at the lunch counter and Dad was sitting right behind me. Nothing much was going on. It was too late for the lunch crowd and too early for the dinner group. Dad and I had made sure that everything was ready for the dinner hour: all the dishes from lunch had been washed and put away; the salt and pepper shakers and sugar bowls had been restocked, the mustard and ketchup bottles refilled; floors swept, bathroom cleaned; food stock returned to full status; and empty napkin containers restored. We were ready, no matter who or what would show its face.

At this point we were simply sitting there catching our breath. Seemingly out of nowhere two figures appeared just outside the large expanse of window that separated the cooking grill from the sidewalk passersby. One, a Black man called Ernie, was dressed in overalls and a long sleeve shirt, a railroad engineer's hat adorning his head. The other man, a Caucasian named Chicago—the only name I'd ever heard him called—wore a short-sleeved shirt, jeans and a woolen pancake hat. Both of them were obviously tipsy, which was their custom. They pressed their faces against the windowpane, first one, then the other, and then did their own version of a dance. Ernie always followed Chicago's lead. Chicago leaned into the window and then, twisting sideways, twirled his hat to the side, saying "Hi, fellas" to us, and then broke away in a stunted pirouette. Ernie followed suit, with nary a variation in his step, then swayed up the street in tandem with Chicago as Dad said, "You see, son, good and bad falls on all the same." No more. Just that. His profundity hung there in the air, huge as a bright harvest moon, just long enough for it to sink into this young man's head. The full understanding moved from my head to my heart as Dad got up, shaking his head compassionately. And we went back to work.

When I was even younger, before Dad returned to restaurant work to help his partner, he was painting at the Bethlehem Steel factory in Lackawanna, a steel city of roughly 53,000 population just south of Buffalo, NY. If either my sister or I got into trouble, or "messed" with my mother, she generally wouldn't handle the situation herself. She'd save the punishment for Dad to dole out. Well, he didn't like this at all, and while I never heard him talk to her about it, he finally took care of it his own way. One day I apparently did something untoward and my mom had sent me to my room with the admonition, "You wait 'til your father gets home. Are you ever going to get it!" I had learned by then that this didn't always mean like how it sounded. I had figured out that sometimes this was meant just to scare my sister or me. My brother Bill was still too young to be concerned about such things. On the other hand, every now and then her words became truth, but I was beginning to discern that Dad didn't like being used as the one to punish. I think, in this case, that giving us a spanking really did hurt him more than it did us—well, maybe—or perhaps this is just an adult thinking that now, not as a less than ten year old, then.

On this one particular day Dad came home from work and Mom launched into an overly dramatic description of what this evil act I had allegedly committed was, and Dad took me down to the basement to distribute the appropriate punishment. When we got there, he whispered, "When I slap the side of my leg, you pretend to cry." No more explanation than that. So he slapped his thigh, and I pretended to cry—two amateur actors, for better or worse. My sister affirms that Dad did the same with her, too. In retrospect, I think sooner or later Mom caught on, but she never said anything to me about it. All I know for sure is that both the threats and spankings ceased soon thereafter. I guess that's all it took to change my ways—and Mom's.

On another occasion, when I was about 16, I was working side by side with Dad, painting houses in the summer to earn money for college. One evening after work and an early dinner, a couple of friends and I went to Dunkirk, a blue-collar town about ten miles away. Our supposed purpose was to go to this one bar where they had a dance band playing every weekend and see if we could pick up some girls. Lee and I were too young to drink, plus I was a dedicated athlete and didn't want to drink. But Bob was 18, and he and Lee decided they wanted to have a gin and tonic. I let myself be talked into risking having one, too, so Bob ordered a round for all of us.

While occasionally sipping the drink, I started feeling a little dizzy, and excused myself to go the men's room. I figured that if I stalled for time, maybe this would wear off, or we'd decide to leave before I had to finish the drink. When I returned, there was a fresh drink in front of all of us. "I didn't want this," I chimed. "Aw, c'mon,

Jimmy boy, this won't hurt you any," Bob chided. Back then I suppose I didn't want any confrontation, or at the very least, I didn't want my friends to think I was some kind of woos, so I let it go. Big mistake!

Again, I sipped faithfully to their purpose. I kept wondering when we were going to try to pick up some of the "chics" (that's what we called them back then), but we never quite got to it.

Sometime later I went, or should I say, staggered, to the bathroom again, this time swearing to myself that I wasn't going to finish this drink. I was beginning to feel sick to my stomach. You guessed it: another fresh drink was waiting for us when I returned. Very long story made short, several drinks later, none ever fully consumed, but collectively amounting to two full drinks— far more than enough for someone who didn't drink—I declared the evening over. I was really getting sick and the place started to spin under me.

Lee and Bob nearly had to carry me out to the car. On the way home I got more and more dizzy, and my stomach was becoming more and more queasy. At one point, I lurched toward the front seat and screamed at the top of my lungs, "STOP, I'M GOING TO THROW UP!" Bob pulled over in the nick of time. How, I'll never know, but by the time Bob stopped I had rolled down the window and, as the car came to a screeching halt, I vomited all down the outside of the car. On some level, I'm sure, I thought that was the least I could do to get even with them.

When they got me home, I had to pee real bad, so I did—right on my front lawn. I think I remember at least gagging some more, maybe even spilling my guts. It's all still such a blur in my memory. I staggered into the house, horrified to see Dad watching the late news on television. I limply waved as I passed him on the way upstairs. He said only, "Good night, Jim." When I got upstairs and looked in the bathroom mirror, I saw an unholy mess: my shirt was spattered with vomit and hanging half out of my pants. My fly was open and part of my shirttail hung out like a limp penis. And my face was as pale as a painted ghost on Halloween night. A fear filled "OH, MY GOD, DAD'S GOING TO KILL ME TOMORROW!" came crashing through in my wildest imagination as I staggered feebly to bed and spun myself into an ugly stupor.

The next thing I remember was Dad calling me to get up for work. I had no earthly idea how I could climb a ladder, let alone sling a six inch brush all day long. But I decided I'd be better off taking my punishment like a man, rather than feigning illness and paying for it later. Well, we went to work and neither of us said much of anything. We prepared the paint, set up our ladders and up the ladders to paint we went. To this day I don't know how I got even one step up off the ground. Befitting our regimen, at about ten o'clock we broke for something to drink. Dad usually carried coffee in his thermos, and I'd have water. When I finally managed to navigate my way down the ladder without falling off, I just sat there like a bump on a log. Dad handed me a glass of juice he had managed to obtain from the grips of the lady of the house. After I had weakly taken a sip or two, Dad interrupted my safe space, saying, "Feeling any better?" Not another word. Not a scolding, not a moral lesson, no chastisement. Nothing. Just, "Feeling any better?" I got the point—real well. It's no wonder I say to this day that my dad was the best man I ever met.

Incidentally, I found out later that week from my so-called friends that while I was in the rest room that first time they had arranged with the waitress for me to continue getting gin and tonics, while their glasses were refilled with just tonic water and lime. I never really did get even with them for this. Nor have I had a gin and tonic since.

Just two other quick stories about Dad and me. He never pried, never asked personal questions—except twice—in my entire time with him. The first time was after I had received my doctorate and was an associate vice president at Buffalo State College. One day when I was visiting Dad in Silver Creek, he asked me after dinner one evening, "Jim, you mind my asking how much money you make now that you have your doctor's degree?" "Not at all, Dad, I make $22,800."

"What?" he replied in astonishment, "That's all you make?"

"Yes, but I really enjoy what I do—after all, you're the one who taught me how to enjoy everything I do."

After what seemed like an interminable pause, Dad followed with this note: "You remember Rob Evans?"

"Sure I do. Why do you ask?" was my rejoinder. "Well," Dad continued in all seriousness, "I just finished painting his place. He's an orthodontist, you know. And he wasn't anywhere near the top of the class like you were. He drives a Mercedes and owns his office building and a lovely home on the lake. And he flies his own airplane. If you'll go back to school and be a dentist, I'll work extra to pay for your schooling. You can't be making only twenty something thousand dollars a year after going to college this long." This from a man who never, to my knowledge, made even that much in a year. Never in all his work life.

The only other time he asked me a personal question was years later, the day after a celebration dinner when I was inaugurated as President of Potsdam College in northern New York. I could not have been happier, not because I had finally "made it" as president, but because both my mom and dad were alive to witness how what they had done in raising me had contributed so richly to reaching this pinnacle in my chosen profession.

On that early spring morning, with frost still melting off the silvered grass and rooftops nearby, we were leisurely sharing a delectable brunch being served in our family room that overlooked the Racquette River as it divided the town into it's very different halves. During a lull in conversation, Dad got up to refill his coffee cup and I joined him in the kitchen. As he poured the cream into his cup—always the cream first, before the coffee—he said, "Mind if I ask you a personal question?" The suddenness struck me like a bump in the night. "No, not at all. Shoot." Well, your mother and I were talking last night, and we wondered—does this job require you to drink?" "Require me to drink? No, why?" "Because after seeing all that the guests at the party drank yesterday, your mother and I grew afraid that you might become an alcoholic." I was stunned by his question, yet moved to glistening eyes by his compassion and sincerity of interest in this matter. "No, Dad, I'm not required to drink. As a matter of fact, I rarely do drink, and when I do it's only a little, because I don't want to put myself in a position of not being in full control of what I'm saying or doing." "Whew, that's good," was his relieved response. "Your mom will be glad to hear that, and so am I." I never heard another word about drinking.

Mom? She was very different from Dad. He was gregarious; she was shy and withdrawn. Dad was nonintrusive; Mom was nosey, pure and simple. She had to know everything that was going on—and why—or why not.

While it was not the style back then for parents to tell you they loved you out loud, I never doubted that either of my parents did love me. Only with Dad, you could feel his love pouring from him full force. He was love itself. Mom? She was much more reserved and you knew her love more by how much she did for you, rather than from any deep connection or emotional outflow. As a matter of fact, it wasn't until much later in life, when I was in my thirties I think, that I regularly began telling my folks that I loved them and gave them a hearty hug. That seemed to release them to regularly respond in a similar fashion. The exchange wasn't really necessary, because I already knew the truth about them loving me, but it was nice to have their love affirmed that way, nonetheless.

When anyone came into Mom's home they could quickly discern a few things: the wonderful, penetrating smell of home baked desserts, like a luscious German chocolate cake or the best chocolate chip cookies in the universe, or the most extraordinary four inch thick lemon or butterscotch pie you ever put into your mouth; flowers and plants caressed you wherever you went; the fireplace in their new home was never used; you could eat off her floors; and the inside and outside of the house took turns being painted on alternate years, just like Virginia, Bill and I took turns taking a bath in the one family bathroom—and always a bath, never a shower. That way there were no tile walls to clean up afterward.

And Mom had the most magnificent yard in town. The lawn looked like the infield in Yankee Stadium: closely mowed in a crosshatched patter, free from debris, so the eyes and soul could reach directly beyond to the flower gardens without interruption. The house was surrounded by textures and colors of an intuitively perfect setting. It was fronted by deep green shrubs that were surrounded by a lush sculpture of shady pachysandra, interrupted now and again with brilliant red geraniums or a patch of multicolored portulaka in the sunny areas. The side garden, which stretched from the front sidewalk all the way behind the house to the garage, was filled with scores of roses of every size, shape and description. The back garden, which flooded back to the fence protecting against a fall over a steep precipice, was likewise candy for the heart's eyes. In summertime people from all over town would come for a walk past the house, hoping either Mom or Dad would invite them for a closer look, actually, to feast on an aesthetic buffet.

Although either Dad or I mowed the lawn and swept and hosed the driveway, it was Mom who always tended the garden. That, like the inside of the house, was her domain, and there was no doubt about it. Just try walking through the door without first taking off your shoes and you'd be sure to find that out. I have to say it was good to learn about cleanliness and order, even if sometimes it felt like just too much. But these ingredients, just like when Mom taught me how to wash and iron and cook, have served me well throughout life, and I'm ever grateful. Yep, she sure was a keeper.

On another level, I always felt Mom held me back some. I could never put my finger on it, but it felt that way nevertheless. While both Mom and Dad supported and encouraged me in what I did, I never felt disappointment from Dad like I did Mom when I didn't achieve exactly what was desired or expected. Now that attitude, much like our own inner critic, can be marvelous when it helps us discern the need to improve and shows us how to do so correctly. But when it even only occasionally beats you down with unreasonable expectations, it can render the soul black and blue. I love her all the same.

Not too long ago, some latent form of resentment about Mom's use of criticism or shame came up in my face. I was photographing rural poverty, meandering to and fro across the back roads of Arkansas. It was a scorcher of a summer. You could see water mirages far ahead on the roads everywhere I went, and even the mosquitoes seemed to have found the air too humid in which to fly. They seemed to be doing a slow backstroke through the water-laden air, adorning hip-waders. Whatever it was that triggered this emotional upsurge I'll probably never know, but I started to get angrier and angrier at Mom. I couldn't seem to stop the downward spiral of emotional venom towards her. I new I didn't normally feel this way about her, and that I loved her deeply, yet somehow I just couldn't seem to break the tide. All at once I heard this inner voice say, "Ask for help." I thought for a moment about that and dismissed it out of hand, thinking "Ask who for what?" Another moment passed and the same voice repeated, "Ask for help." Ah, I got it this time. I had learned to listen to my intuition and to be obedient to its voice, no matter how unusual the message might have seemed, but had been steered off course momentarily by my feelings of anger and resentment.

In the next breath, I sought inwardly, "I need some help here. I need just one simple reminder of why I love Mom so much." Not a half-minute later I came around a bend in this dusty county road and found myself full flush with bed after bed of bright flowers: chrysanthemums of all colors, bright orange marigolds, brilliant purple and pink cosmos, you name them. I thought for a moment that I had died and gone to flower heaven. Their perfectly composed hues and tones brought tears to my eyes and took my breath away, sort of like seeing one of my newborn children for the first time, or the feeling I got inside the first time I thought I had fallen in love. And this resonated with the authenticity of my love for my real first love on this planet: Mom. The gratitude I felt was indescribable, the gratitude for what she taught me about the beauty of flowers and colors and textures, all which were but life's manifestations of the beauty she was. And suddenly, from the same sacred place from which those gilded words had guided me just moments ago, the gratitude for life itself filled me to the brim.

I mentioned that mom was shy. She was so shy that her brothers used to tease her without let up. Or maybe it was the other way around, I don't know. I remember so many times when Uncle Bill, Uncle Eddie or Uncle Stanley (Mom was one of six in a first generation Polish family), one or the other, or in rapid serial fashion, would tease her about the "ants" in her banana bread, or the "bunny droppings" in her toll house cookies.

Then they'd start in with the Polish jokes. Mom didn't take to them too well. As a matter of fact, she found them downright rude and didn't buy into the argument her brothers made that it was okay for a "Polock" to tell Polish jokes on themselves. It wasn't until her later years that she began to see this cause with different eyes, so to speak. Apparently my sister Virginia had taken it upon herself to reframe the issue somehow. It doesn't really matter how it happened, it just did.

I'll never forget the first time Mom told me a Polish joke. I was so astonished I didn't laugh. I think her feelings were hurt. After I recovered, we told a few to each other and all was well again. Mom had taken on a sense of humor of her own, and perhaps became a little less prideful in the process. One thing I'll tell you: it warmed my heart to see her laugh, and it was even more delightful to see that slightly mischievous look in her eye as she got ready to tell us one.

To me, Mom and Dad seemed inseparable. When they finally got to build their own house, the last one they owned, they had a minister build it. I was married and living elsewhere at the time, and from time to time I'd visit, both to be in their company, but also to see how the house was coming along. The minister only had one eye, but was one of the best carpenters I have ever seen. A true artist, he custom-made every cupboard and fashioned every nook and cranny in that house.

Every brick was placed just right, all square angles were perfect, each fireplace stone was set as it should be. Each night at work's end—and, it was nightfall, not five o'clock in the afternoon, for Mr. Munson worked long days—he'd go to Mom and Dad's rental place up the street before he left and read the Bible with them. Such reverence became a habit and more and more frequent were the times thereafter when I'd find them putting the day to bed in the Word.

Also, Mom never learned to drive, so everywhere she went she either had to walk, or she'd wait until Dad came home from work and then they'd go grocery shopping or play bingo after having dinner out. Oh, my, did Mom ever like to play bingo, and she often won; probably not as often as she said she did, but I'd been with her when she did win several times at one sitting. In hindsight, this dependency she had on Dad to drive her everywhere could have easily been a codependency, and Dad never seemed to mind it all. He seemed to cherish it—and her—above all. Perhaps instead of codependency it was simply being in love and loving whatever you do with the one you love. They both taught that very well.

Earlier I referred to my first inauguration. You remember. It was when Dad had asked me the personal question about drinking. Well, two months to the day after that, Dad died. I'd rather put it that he'd moved on to teach spiritual storytelling to the angels. He went as he wanted, though. He once told Virginia three things he wanted about his death. The first was that he would die working. The second was that he wanted a closed casket. The third was that he wanted the Masons to be present at his wake. Dad fell off a ladder, still painting at 78 years young, mind you, and died almost instantly of a fractured skull. Because of the fracture, there was immense swelling, so his body was not shown. Despite early protestations by the local priest to the contrary, we finally got clearance for his Mason friends to have a separate ceremony for Dad. And the last time anyone saw him alive, he was standing at the foot of his ladder telling stories and laughing with some passersby.

There are no words to convey the depth of what I then called my loss. Since then I have counted the blessings this extraordinary man brought into my life over and over again. They matched and even exceeded the gratitude I felt all my life for his giftedness to me. I hope I've picked up even a few of his wonderful ways.

About four years later I was inaugurated as Chancellor of the University of Arkansas at Little

Rock, AR. My sister and mother were dumbfounded by my move from upstate New York to the South. I don't think it mattered to Bill one wit, except for missing one another. I seem to recall that both Mom and Virginia envisioned Arkansas as a hillbilly state, filled with barefoot, corncob pipe smokers. I had wanted Mom to consider moving to Arkansas to live, but she still was very attached to the house that she and Dad had made home. Plus she wasn't at all sure of what she'd find in this rural Southern state. Both she and Virginia attended the inauguration and related festivities and found their preconceptions to be hugely erroneous.

For me, the most profound highlight of that occasion, actually I can honestly say of my entire time in Arkansas, over a decade in all, was a seemingly innocent happening. Bill Clinton, then governor, was the featured luncheon speaker following the installation event. As usual, he was witty, brilliant, entertaining, captivating, and sweeping in his knowledge of the university and how it was contributing to the general welfare of his state. After lunch, as was the usual procedure, his secret policeman came up behind Governor Clinton and simply touched him lightly on the shoulder to let him know it was time to move on. Bill turned to me and said, "Jim, is there anything I can do to make this even more special for you?" Can you imagine? After thanking him profusely for what he already had done, I had the temerity to say, "There is one, very brief thing that would put the finishing touch on it all. Could you take just a minute to say a word or two to my mother and mother-in-law?" "Of course I will," he responded with his usual social generosity, and off he went. After taking not a minute, but a full ten minutes with each of them, he gracefully departed—with my unending gratitude in tow. As I looked over at Mom and my mother-in-law, their faces were beaming from ear to ear.

Little did I know at the time how even more grateful I would become to Governor Clinton for that one kind gesture. Several days later I called Mom to see how her return trip went and how she was doing generally. She seemed to still be grieving and missing Dad a lot. I was coming to understand what it meant to have your heart broken by the death of a loved one. Observing her was that clear a lesson in itself. We got to talking about the inauguration and what fun she and Virginia had. And how impressed they both were by the reality of Arkansas, in contrast to myth, that is.

Then, out of nowhere, she offered this: "You know, Jim, I've been thinking a lot about your suggestion that I move to Arkansas, and I might just do it." I was dumbfounded by this turnabout in attitude and preference. "How come?" was about all I could muster as I held myself back from becoming too excited until I could see something real come of it. "Well, Virginia and I were talking today, and I thought, "What a wonderful state Arkansas must be to live in, if the governor could take ten minutes of his busy schedule to make me feel important, and I don't even live there. Here, in New York, the governor has so many state policemen surrounding him you can't get close enough to even see what he really looks like." Whew! I was blown away by her deep realization. I never got to see her newfound dream fulfilled, though, for she died exactly two months after the occasion of my inauguration. I think it must have been from a broken heart.

I'm not ashamed to say that I have invested a good bit of my life since then completing the accumulative grieving process over their departure. I feel so blessed to have had them take me "on loan." They were absolutely the best.

There was yet another special something I learned about each of them, but not until after they had gone to the Great Beyond. I vividly recall the stories.

One sunny early afternoon I found myself sitting with all the relatives that remained on my father's side in the sunlit back yard of my cousin Stavros and his family who lived in Epanomi, a small village outside Thessaloniki, Greece. I speak very little Greek, just enough to be dangerous, I'm accustomed to saying. And most of my Greek relatives speak little or no English. That day one of my other cousins, Tasos, from Athens, was my translator. Dad was the only male of six children, and what was left of his sisters were actively participating in rapt conversation with one another. There was diminutive Aunt Eleni, then 88, and hearty like a fifty year old; Aunt Tasoula, then 86, sipping on a glass of white wine and puffing away on a cigarette like a teenager trying out her first pack of weeds; and, then of course, there was elegant Aunt Artemis from Athens, 84 and sprite as I was, full of fun and games.

At one point I became curious about how Dad came to leave Greece, so I asked Tasos to inquire of our aunts what had caused him to leave. He asked, and they chatted a bit about it until he turned to say, "They want to know your version first." "Well," I responded, "Dad always told the story this way. When he was about 15 or so he got on an ocean liner in the harbor in Thessaloniki to visit with a friend who was a merchant marine. His friend showed him around the ship at great length and they got so involved in doing so that the ship had set out to sea without them being aware of it. As the story goes, he stowed away under the tarp of an emergency vessel until they could figure out a way to make it legitimate for him to be there. Needless to say, they got caught, so they put Dad to good use doing odd jobs around the ship. Eventually they put him to work in the galley. I recall Dad telling me that he used to wear a ring of garlic around his neck to ward off sickness aboard ship. He sailed around the world a few times before landing for good in the Brooklyn Naval Yards, where he began his life in America. The long and short of it is that he never went back home, afraid that his father would severely punish him for being such a bad boy." All along Tasos was translating the story I was telling. All the women and, by now, all the rest of the family who were gathered around the picnic tables, were enraptured by the goings-on.

As Tasos finished my version of the story, my aunts laughed uproariously in unison. "What's going on?" I inquired of Tasos. He asked what was so funny, and after a fashion he, too, laughed. Everyone was amused at something I had not yet been made privy to. "Well," continued Tasos, "your aunts say that's not really what happened. They think it's funny that your father told the story different from what actually triggered it all. You see, your grandfather was, I think you would say it, a stern man; very stern. He was always after uncle Aristides to be a doctor, but your father didn't want any part of that. One day he and his father had a big argument about it and your father ran away from home. They didn't hear from him until a few months later, when he finally wrote to say he simply had stowed away on the ship, vowing never to return home." He never did.

On Mom's part, well, it was during the viewing of her body in a local chapel on the evening before her funeral that I was alerted to a long-standing family secret. Family and friends were gathered, sitting around and reminiscing about times long since passed. At one point in conversations with my aunts and uncles (Mom was also one of six, with two sisters and three brothers, all remaining at the time) I mentioned something about wanting to visit Helena, Montana, one day, where Mom had said she was born. "Helena, what does that have to do with anything?" inquired Aunt Gene. "Well, Mom always said she was born in Helena, that's all." With a laugh Aunt Gene said, "No, that's not true at all. She was born in nearby Roundup, but she never wanted anyone to know that. Can you imagine, being born in a place with a name like Roundup? Gert was too embarrassed to admit she was born there, that's all."

The collective enjoyed the exchange to no end, and other stories began to be spun, one after another, like how, every week during the depression, Mom and Dad would bring sacks of food from town out to my grandmother's farm in Forestville, some five miles away. And how Aunt Connie, who used to work in Dad's restaurant with Mom, had a crush on Dad, but Mom had won his heart instead. On and on it went. Years later, while visiting a friend in Montana, I got to check out Mom's story for myself. Yes, she was a woman from Roundup.

Early on I said that I believed that one of the main reasons we come to this planet is to actually become the stories that will inform and inspire others to be what they really are: lovers of the first order. Sure as cotton, Mom and Dad became their stories. And, just as sure, they had proved without a shadow of doubt that they were lovers of the first order.

In fact, I can see Mom and Dad in that light even now: Mom grooming Heaven's gardens with the beauty she is, and Dad entertaining with wisdom the angelic array of love painters. I think my grieving is finally finished. I'll continue celebrating their lives instead.

I'll confess one last thing. Some years back, after first losing Dad, and then Mom, each precisely two months after an inaugural installation ceremony, I decided irrevocably that I would never again be inaugurated.

I have only a brother and sister left, and I'm not going to risk losing them that way.

WE HAVE MET THE ENEMY

It's a balmy late afternoon in Cardenas, Cuba. The late afternoon light paints all forms of life with its warm, golden palette. I have a few hours until the dinner hour while my friends from the Plowshares Institute relax after conducting an intensive two-day seminar on conflict transformation.

The refurbishing breeze from the Caribbean gently caresses the organic nature that fills my camera's viewfinder with layer upon layer of street life. Scores of bicycles are adorned by young and old alike. Horse drawn taxis carrying their cargoes of people alongside construction materials. An occasional truck spews tell tale blue smoke from the combustion of diesel fuel. A seemingly endless array of colorful Chevys, Fords, and Dodges from a bygone era punctuate the scene, motored largely by Russian engines that replaced the originals during the heyday of USSR-Cuban collaboration. Uniformed students awaiting rides via carriages, bicycles, buses, whatever, gaily engage one another in activity only teenagers can stir.

Figures of the less well to do weave their way toward the tiny shadow-filled window. A few fresh-baked rolls transported on the end of a feminine chestnut colored hand exchange for a handful of ration stamps. Spirited conversations fill the air from every direction as gaggles of youngsters harbor around the pay phones like sentinels guarding against intrusion from the likes of the adult male patiently awaiting his turn, arms neatly folded across his belly, a knowing smile adorning his face.

The entire scene captivates my imagination, etching indelible images on the lining of my heart while playing out the alchemy of the black and white film that rolls its way toward completion. I am becoming drunk on the inspirational imagery of relationship.

I am suddenly taken by the insertion of a well-maintained 1957 Chevy sedan, which has found its way to my side. It brings a smile to my heart as I recall the replica of its salmon and silver body in my ex-mother in law's driveway years ago. Privately I wonder if it brings its owner as much pleasure as that one provided for her. My dream of times past is pleasantly interrupted by a flow of horse drawn buggies approaching from all sides. Their converging motion is compelling and I bring the viewfinder up to my eye to frame the timing in just the right configuration, with a blend of bicycles weaving in and out of the image and children forging their way amidst it all. It is frantic, yet symbolic of a world-class ballet, beautifully choreographed in its display of each disparate, yet collaborative element, each contributing perfectly to a more complete whole. Stories within a story are everywhere, writing themselves.

While creating a few images of this variety, I notice at the left edge of my viewfinder a uniformed Cuban policeman approaching in my general direction, and include him in an image or two, adding stark contrast to the softer canvas of life. I immediately forget his presence and continue the forage into this forest of living activity. A moment or two later, I really have no idea how much time has transpired, the policeman approaches me and asks if I speak Spanish. For just an instant, I think I'm a goner, but then realize I haven't done anything wrong, so simply relax into the moment, awaiting what it is sure to offer me. I remember saying to myself, "There is only Life, thus room for nothing else, especially fear." In an instant the peace that comes with Truth fills me beyond description, and its grace carries me through the entire incident.

I tell the officer that I don't speak Spanish, and ask if he can speak English. His response echoes mine. I motion him across the street to my living quarters, indicating as best I can that we might well find a translator there. As we start across the main street, a huge bus almost takes us with it, and I pull him back by the arm, obviously the right thing to do in a humanitarian sense—even if

it did instantaneously dawn on me that he could have just as easily taken my action as an aggressive one and shot me dead on that spot. Fortunately for both of us, I quickly point out the fast-approaching vehicle and he seems to understand the positive nature of my act.
As we cross the street, another gentleman, in plain clothes, an Afro-Cuban about 6 feet 4 inches tall, and a certain muscular 250 pounds, joins us. I motion to the building we are approaching, hoping he got the idea that we're headed for some help with translation. As soon as we clear the archway into the building, I ask the hostess if she is bilingual. She responds in the negative, which gives Plainclothes the impetus to ask, in perfect English I might add, where I am from. When I answer the United States, he asks me for my passport. I say that I'll have to go to my room to get it, reflecting in my best broken Spanish, "Un momento, por favor," motioning upstairs with a wave, closing with,"Hasta pronto" just for the fun of it.

On the way upstairs I decide to leave my camera in the room, and do so, gathering my passport and visa as requested. When I return, my escorts begin recording information from the documents. Just then a woman strides through the foyer, and the hostess asks if she speaks English. She says that she does, and proceeds to speak with the policemen. Turning to me she asks in broken English, but in much better terms than my fractured Spanish, what I've been doing and where I'm staying. I tell her I'm staying at this domicile and that I've been involved in a two day workshop in conflict transformation, chuckling inwardly at the irony, and that I was simply taking a few minutes before the dinner hour to photograph people on the streets, just as I had done yesterday.

I am puzzled by her explanation and respond that people are my specialty, not houses, and that the She relays my message to the policemen and turns to me saying, "Well, they say you've been photographing for two days and that you've taken pictures of the alien's house."

The only house I can recall photographing was one with a green 1947 Ford in front of it, but there were no people in the vicinity of the car at the time. She conveys that to the gentlemen and returns to me with the now familiar, "They say you've been taking pictures of the alien's house, and you're not supposed to do that" or at least that's what I heard her say. Again, I rejoin by asking her what she means by an alien's house, "I don't know what you mean by an alien's house." "No," she responds in a new understanding of the situation, "not an alien's house, Elian's house."

"Alien who?" I ask, absolutely confounded by the conversation.

"Elian Gonzalez," she says, "you know, the little boy who lost his mother on the way from Cuba to the United States." Like the key piece of a picture puzzle falling neatly into place to save the day, all the fragments suddenly fit together.

"Elian Gonzalez lives here, in Cardenas?" I ask, bewildered by the enormity of realization.

"Yes," she says, "just up the street, and they don't want you to take pictures of him."

"I thought he lived in Havana," I said, "and didn't have any idea he was here, or where he might live. I wouldn't want to invade his space in any event."

"Translator" conveys my explanation to the police and they remain noncommittal in both words and deportment, still hunching over my passport and visa, continuing to record information.

At that moment, a middle-aged Cuban woman who had been taking all this in speaks up in Spanish. From her demeanor, I can't tell which side she's on, so I just wait patiently for Translator to tell me what's going on. When the speaker finishes, Translator turns to me and says that the speaker was vouching for me, indicating that she had seen me photograph on both days and that I was only photographing people in their normal travels of the day. I thank her for her input, hoping that it helped the situation. After a brief drop in the conversation, Plainclothesman turns toward me and hands me back my papers, saying in perfect English, "There's no problem." He says something else to Translator in Spanish and turns to leave. "Muchas gracias y mucho gusto," I say to the plainclothesman in the best way I know how, and shake his hand. He turns to leave without comment. I repeat the same to the uniformed officer and the empty response repeats itself.

Those that remain take a communal deep breath, followed by some chatting among the three women. Translator turns to me saying that the plainclothesman is Elian's private, 24 hour a day, bodyguard, and that he said that it would be okay for me to photograph in the direction facing away from Elian's house. I allow that I am finished for the day, as the daylight was drawing to a close, and thanked everyone for their helpful assistance. Translator closes by saying that just two weeks ago a European was video-graphing Elian's house and was intercepted by the police and not only solidly reprimanded, but they confiscated his video equipment as well. If I hadn't already felt fortunate, that made me feel all the more so.

I reflect on this incident throughout the evening (and have frequently since) and share it with my friends and our host over dinner. They chid me about having been a malvadito (a little mischief maker) the whole trip, and that it would have been simple justice if I had been taken to jail for the evening. I play along with them, but can't help but think about the horrendous conditions Elian must have to live under, with no real freedom from the potential for invasion into his privacy. And that we in the United States, Cuban Americans and all, who made such a political game of Elian's distressful situation, are the real aliens in the domain of humanitarianism.

In a large way, I can't help but reflect upon all the conflicting information we have been fed, by Cuban and American sources alike, and wonder what the truth of the matter really is. From my photographic episodes over twelve days I have come to see people and circumstances that both confirm and deny that information—mostly confirming the information conveyed by everyday Cubans and denying that distributed by our agencies at home and their agencies in Cuba.

Studies by independent, nonpartisan agencies and foundations in the United States indicate that the embargo policy our government imposed more than half century ago is a failed one. Generally, the Cuban people see the embargo as morally wrong, yet clearly acknowledge the difference between the policies of our government and concern of its people. The consensus seems to indicate that if the United States really wants to oust Fidel, the most advantageous way would be to change our policy to one of purposeful engagement. Programs similar to those that have worked with other nations suggest reestablishing commercial relations, beginning with food and medicine and proceeding to two-way trade; actively encouraging academic, scientific and cultural exchanges, and permitting travel by any US citizen; exploring collaborative programs dealing with antiterrorism, migration, drug interdiction and common environmental concerns; and increasing the level of diplomatic contacts and encouraging Cuba to relax restrictions on freedom of association and expression.

If we were to drop the embargo and begin investing in the Cuban people in more humanitarian ways, they would perhaps be more willing to modify the Cuban government in order to have a higher quality of life and live more fully productive ones. As long as Cubans see our government as the primary enemy, however, they will not rise up against Castro. Simply put, when we change the way we see such things, the things we see will change.

President George W. Bush recently exacerbated the economic situation by tightening the 44-year embargo, the stated intent being to further reduce the amount of hard currency available to Cubans, thus supposedly putting more heat on Castro. To all but the most naive, the primary intent employed by the current administration is to strengthen the Florida Cuban-American vote for the upcoming election. As long as we continue to see and act politically instead of spiritually, such policies are doomed to failure in the larger scope of life.

The one thing that carries me though all the confliction is the disarming nature of the Cuban people. They are spiritual beings who know how to, and do, celebrate life for the gift it is. They are generally happy people despite their dire financial circumstances and heartily demonstrate their strong character and generosity of spirit. And they seem reconciled with God. This oneness plays out in a sense of hope and an aura of inner peace and joy that are generally difficult to find in people of far greater means.

As the famous poet-philosopher Pogo once said, "We have met the enemy and he is us." Perhaps enlightened leadership will one day end this failed policy so the dreams and needs of the Cuban people can be fulfilled at last, despite their government—and ours. It is time we stopped belittling people with our oppressive political strength and instead uplift them with the power of our loving spirit. Nothing could do more to validate respect for the sacredness of human dignity.

THANKS FOR THE YELLOW ROSES

My heart is pounding on the back of my shirt pocket, my eyes moist like the morning dew on the freshly spun earth fairies that blessed my walking meditation earlier this morning. Stirred by faint renderings of sadness, yet buoyed by its mixture with the heartfelt joy of relational healing, I am forever grateful in the memory of the past few days. Memories often do that for me in these times.

Usually my heart opens like the Grand Canyon, embracing the light of yet another day at the seat of compassion. Today is no exception. My three sons and two daughters are converging on their mother, Jackie, my late, former wife, for a four-day weekend. Grace appears to have taken over her life now.

I am a firm believer in miracles. Not just the spectacular, heroic kind most people call miracles, but more especially those that simply appear when we are really paying attention. Jackie and I spawned these five wonderful young people we are both proud of, separately and, I strongly suspect, together, as well—that is, if we ever gave ourselves the opportunity to join our feelings in this regard.

Jackie was diagnosed with terminal cancer nearly three years ago and given no more than six months to live. She is so strong-willed and so committed to her children and grandchildren that she won't leave until she sees that they're just as she thinks they ought to be. That time has just about arrived.

Jackie has some good days and some not so good. At this point, she is weak and has sporadic recollection of people and time, splicing pieces of her history into a cinematic production that makes sense to perhaps only her. It doesn't matter, really, who else understands. The only thing that does matter is that beyond all her pain and suffering she seems to be at peace with life; it is that which regularly fills the air with angelic giftedness lately. Today is a case in point.

I am heading to the NW Arkansas airport to pick up Alison, our older daughter, and Todd, twin to Dana Lynn, our youngest. On the way I stop to pick up a few vittles for home at a specialties market nearby. As I near the checkout counter I notice a large display of fresh flowers and stop to drink them in. I have a passion for flowers that turns me into a compulsive shopper: I can't buy only a single plant or bouquet of flowers if my life depended on it.

My deepest self says I should take Jackie some. I learned long ago to follow my intuition, so I begin to make a judgment as to which kind I should purchase. Just as suddenly as I was admonished to take flowers to Jackie, I am led to bunches of effervescent roses. The variety of colors is breathtaking and choices abound. I particularly like the soft white ones, with a blush of peach on the underbelly. But this is not to be, for my intuition speaks loud and clear once again: "Take her the yellow ones." I smile and pull out the best of those for Jackie and, true to myself, also take a bunch of the white ones for home. I pay my bill and head off to the airport.

Instead of heading directly to Fayetteville, Alison, Todd and I head to a nice place for lunch and talk about everything but the impending visit. It's obvious by the deflection tactics they're using that both Todd and Alison are uneasy about being in such painful space, seemingly watching in their mind's eye the life bleed from their mother, bit by painful bit.

All at once a suggestion, a question actually, blurts out of my mouth: "Your mother likes movies doesn't she, Alison?"

"Yes, she sure does," she responds.

"Well, I know she likes to laugh and I'll bet she hasn't done that in awhile. How about you all taking her to a funny movie, like "My Big Fat Greek Wedding?"

"I saw that, it was a howl," Alison laughs, "a great idea, Dad."

We talk about how it might be better for Jackie to spend her remaining time doing what she really enjoys. Watching a good movie might make her tired, but at least she'd get tired doing what she likes rather than from just sitting in bed thinking about her demise. We agree that it should be done and with that, we depart for Fayetteville.

Upon arrival, Todd and Alison enter the front door without ringing the bell, as if it were home. I follow closely, but tentatively, for I have not been invited into Jackie and Bobbie's house before. As we enter, Jackie spins her wheelchair around to greet them. Hugs and kisses of welcome fill the air. It does my heart good to see her looking so good. I haven't' seen Jackie in months, and she looks surprisingly healthy for all she's been through.

In the larger scope of things I just let life happen and follow Todd and Alison's lead. Being a natural hugger, I wrap my arms around Jackie and she hugs me back as I plant a kiss on her cheek. As we part, I hand her the roses.

"Are these for me?" she asks excitedly.

"Yep," I respond, not knowing what would come next.

"Oh, Jim," she beams, "you remembered! Yellow roses are my favorite!"

Holding her heart in mine, I feel the pain of our past shift dramatically. Tears form into tributaries as we both release to the grace of new beginnings, and she initiates, for the very first time in over 17 years, "Jim, why don't you sit for awhile? The kids are all here and it would be nice if you could." I don't even have to think about my answer. Feeling the joy in the glow of the moment, I hear myself say something foolish like, "Well, all right then," and relax myself into a nearby chair to watch the rest of this homemade drama.

Just the other day, Jackie told Mark, our second oldest and Jackie's self-designated caretaker for over 15 months now, that she had a dream about her and Jesus. Jesus had her try on shoes and after exhausting the supply, He told her that she had very narrow feet and He would have to go find just the right shoes for her. He'd return with them in short order, He affirmed, and the dream ended. And just a night or two from now she'll be telling her family gathering around the supper table how pleased she is that they are all there together, that she loves them to no end, that they mean everything to her. Then she'll say something like, "Well, I'm leaving soon, very soon, so if any of you have anything you want to say to me in private, you'd better do it while you're here, because you won't get another chance."

This anecdote helps me know how much courage this woman really has—by this time she's made of courage, actually. And it makes her live in her private truth now. I suspect that everyone was awakened to their own in this moment of the new reality.

Times are pretty tense and sadness fills the air. Throughout the day, each of our children confesses a fear or pain to me, all in their own timing, all in their own way. All I can do is encourage them to sit with their feelings and let it take them to their own meaning on the other side. One way or another, they know I'm there for them.

The tenderness of these moments takes me to my own private depths, and sadness, merged with extraordinary gratitude for what we have had together as a family, and since, paints my canvas of life in the richest hues of love.

When I get home, I call Mark to tell him of my latest intuitive "hit." "Mark, what do you think about creating some photographs of all of you with your mother? That way, after some of you have left for home, she can have the photos to remind her of the good times you've had." "Sounds good to me, Dad. I'll ask Mom what she thinks and call you back." He calls back almost immediately, and says to bring my cameras over the next afternoon. I am elated at the opportunity that this gift affords.

When I arrive, Alison is primping Jackie, and everyone but Kevin, our oldest son who was Jackie's live-in caregiver for months before Mark quit his job to spell him, and Bobbie, Jackie's husband, are gathered for the event. Kevin soon arrives from work, but Bobbie has a pressing engagement he can't break.

We gather on the front verandah and I begin to photograph, assembling various configurations as I'm prompted. Seemingly out of nowhere, Cheri, Jackie's sister, tells me to get in a picture with Jackie and our children. I beg off, feeling privately that it wouldn't be a good idea to have a photo with me and them without Bobbie there to do the same. I am admonished to get with it and reluctantly obey. We finish the session with Alison suggesting a photo with the children and just me. We all gather on and around the porch swing nearby.

I tell everyone that I'm going to take the film to get it processed so everyone can have copies of favorites before they return home. As I head off, they gather Jackie and take her to the movies. A smile embraces my heart at the good news.

When I return with the photos later that afternoon, Jackie is resting in the aftermath of what turned out to be a fun-filled time for her. Everyone agrees that as long as Jackie can handle it, this kind of activity is what should be continued.

I distribute the photos to everyone and excited bantering about one photo or another fills the air. During a slight pause in the action, Todd holds up the photo of everyone with Jackie and me and announces wistfully, "Dad—this one is the miracle picture." Time is pregnant with pause and tears glisten simultaneously in our eyes. The others silently affirm the truth of that proclamation. Immersed in the salve of this loving moment, I know that on some deeper level we are healed of the darkness imprisoned by the distant past. My heart fills with gratitude to such a degree that I feel it will burst.

Now a week later, I take three copies of the black and white photo of Jackie and the children over to Mark. I have just mailed copies to Alison, Todd and Dana Lynn. I knock softly at Jackie's front door in case she is napping. Sure enough, Mark comes to the door and, motioning with his forefinger to his mouth, he lets me know our conversation needs to be taken out onto the front verandah. I give the framed photos for Jackie, Kevin and Mark to him, explaining that I'm running late for a dental appointment, so he says he'll call me in a day or so to catch up on things. We exchange our usual hugs and "I love you's" and I depart as announced.

Today Mark calls and asks how I feel. I've been suffering for a few days with a debilitating case of sciatica and have slept for only a few hours each night. My voice conveys this energetic emptiness and Mark shows concern by the intonation and inflection of his questions. In response I put him at as much ease as I can muster. After all, he has been running on empty for months now since he began nearly around the clock personal care for Jackie, so I don't need to add to his misery. Having received some assurance that I will get past this in good shape, he tells me that Jackie loved the picture. "You know what Mom said about you, Dad?"

"I can't even begin to imagine, Mark."

"Well, she said: Your father's getting to be a sweet old man."

Stunningly, grace falls silent.

THE JEWEL IN THE LOTUS

I had just begun a new book, new to me that is; an enlightening piece on creative meditation by Grace Cooke. She illumines with teachings from White Eagle, the same Indian spiritual teacher that brings Jesus the Christ to light in the most profound understanding of that which comes to us from investing ourselves in meditation. I have no earthly idea why I am suddenly moved away from this intriguing look at meditation, a critical pathway to the inner straits of the divine, but I am. Actually, the truth of it for me is that it's not some earthly idea that has created my movement, but rather the inordinate power of inspiration that has me now at this computer keyboard.

Just a dozen pages into this moving account of meditational bliss, a distant but nonetheless profound memory comes to light. Its power is that compelling. The events that led to the tale took place on the Milford Track, one of many stunning walking trails on the south island of New Zealand, some 32 miles over what is known as the Southern Alps. My then spouse, Helen Jane, and I had committed to this adventure as part of our trip to honor her childhood dream of visiting Australia in all its splendor. As we traversed the tropical jungle floor along exotic and simple flower-bordered pathways, with backpacks carrying little more than the bare essentials strapped to our backs, not unlike burros trudging across the mountains to Machu Picchu, I couldn't help thinking that nothing in life's green acre could be any more beautiful than this.

We trekked only a few miles the first night, just to gather with the other thirty or so others who had a similar agenda. Even that little jaunt filled my lungs with the freshest air I had breathed in years, and my heart filled to the brim with heavenly anticipation. After dinner that first night, we were paired with another couple for the remainder of the trip.

For three nights we were to be bunkmates and, as it often turns out, we became fast, lifelong friends. They were an English couple who spoke kind of funny, like we sounded to them, I'm sure. They both had a great sense of humor and were sterling conversationalists. The man of the couple was a tease, and liked to pull everyone's leg. His wife, a sensible, plain-speaking woman of great character, would simply smilingly shake her head in what had now become accustomed acceptance of his shenanigans. But none of this really has anything to do with the real essence of the story.

On the morning of our last day together, we had a warm, filling breakfast, with extraordinarily yummy homemade oatmeal, eggs, crisp bacon, and all the trimmings. On this day we were set to descend from the last of the mountains and my legs were achingly testifying to what felt like unseemly abuse afflicted by the hundreds of sharp rocks and slippery boulders. My calves and the bottoms of my feet were on fire and crying for relief.

Of course, the real testimony was to being out of shape for such a challenging activity as this one, and I was challenged, at least momentarily, to restructure my physical training regimen upon returning home so this would never, ever, happen again. As is often the case, the challenge left as quickly as it had appeared, caused by an internal reminder that I needn't train for mountain climbing if I didn't intend to mountain climb again.

As we began down the last of the loose shale-strewn paths, I stopped momentarily to create a few memorable images with my camera—as though the ones that were already etching themselves on the lining of my heart wouldn't be enough. I paused to replace the cover on my lens, knowing the footing would be uneasy, at best, and I didn't want to damage the lens on my camera should I have a spill.

In no longer than it took for this thought to leave my mind, I caught my toe on the edge of a rock and felt the weight of my knapsack flip me over, head over heals, landing on a huge boulder along the very edge of a recent rock slide. Had it not been for that boulder stopping me, I could easily have flipped over the side, tumbling a few hundred feet below. My half summersault completed itself with my knees slashing across other boulders on the way down, and my head crashed to an abrupt halt on the boulder that saved my very life. To say I was stunned is a gross misrepresentation. Helen Jane rushed to my aid, or so I thought, but all I heard her say was something like, "Is it okay if I take your picture?" Apparently I hadn't heard her ask if I was right with the world. Good thing I wasn't of clear mind then, or my response might have been different from the one I delivered in a somewhat groggy state: "I think I'm okay. I just need a minute or so to collect myself."

The most compelling thought running through my mind was how utterly clumsy it was of me to let that happen. I sometimes get self-critical when I'm really tired, and came to a quick understanding of both realizations. After bandaging my throbbing knees and giving my aching head a bit of comfort with a ready-made ice pack, we began afresh on our downward trek with only my badly bruised ego still to attend to.

Disgust with myself began to rear its head again, and I heard this little voice inside me, that often saves me from myself, say: "Let yourself see how a pack mule would traverse this steep decline." Obedient to the command, I asked for the vision and it wasn't a split second before the imaginary National Geographic scene unfolded. True to the nature of this beast of burden, he stepped carefully first with one foot, slid it over the rock until it felt firm, and then stepped with the other front foot, repeating the pattern time and time again. Slowly, but surely, he felt his way down the slope. The donkey, even as experienced as he was, knew it was a treacherous descent and didn't rush a thing about it.

The even more spooky part of all this was that I came to see *myself* as that pack animal. Indeed, I had become the animal as I watched myself on the descent, placing one step carefully after another, taking the same precautions he would have under similar conditions. In the midst of all this I heard a self-realization burst into presence: "Wow, if this beast of burden was this cautious and aware of the danger, how could I expect more of myself than this expert?" All at once my highly self-critical self let up on me, and I felt an almost instantaneous burst of inner confidence—and praise for waking up to the absolute truth of the matter, rather than bathing myself in self-pity and disgust any longer. A real teacher this donkey was. As a willing student, I replicated the earlier guidance provided by the inner imagery for the remaining part of the descent, striking the last steps of the decline now completely at peace with myself.

When we got to the bottom of the mountain we stepped onto a several mile stretch of a narrow, winding path, matted with thousands of sharp, angular stone chips. My heart sank. It didn't take more that a few steps before I heard others, both in front and back of me, whining about how their feet were in such pain that they didn't know how they'd make it to the very end. My feet and legs echoed their sentiments exactly, and I asked inwardly for strength in the form of a way to relieve the pain.

No longer than it took to place one pained foot in front of another, a handsome, black-haired, dark-eyed, Native Indian, adorned only in a breechcloth and moccasins, appeared in my mind's eye off to the right. His expression was one that usually accompanies a dry sense of humor, with a slight smile turned up at the corners of his mouth and a glint in his eye. I could hear his voice—my own inner-vision voice, of course—as he shook his head from side to side, feigning utter disbelief: "Oh, you palefaces make things so dramatic—simply let the moss be your feet." His words awakened me to the obvious all around me. On both sides of the path for as far as I could see were the most gorgeous carpets of lush, rich-green moss. I stepped off to the side of the path and felt as though someond had affixed giant pillows to the bottoms of my feet. Needless to say, I had no trouble making it to the end of the trek. I felt immense gratitude—and thanked my new Indian friend—for the wisdom that saved me from the pain of my own shortsightedness and self-pity.

Now, years later, I have come to the full understanding of those episodes: the jewel in the lotus is the inner understanding that comes from putting one's full faith in the inner Voice—and that alone.

And then being obedient to the grace which is our sufficiency in all matters and circumstances.

. THE TRUTH THAT QUICKENS

They, whoever they is, used to call the last Monday in May Memorial Day something else, I don't remember what, with all the changes in such things these days. Maybe I even have it all backwards. Politically correct they call it. Why don't we just do away with the "they's" instead? That would make life simpler and just as much sense in the long run.

Anyway, for my money it's Memorial Day 2003. Friend and brilliant photographer Siegfried and I have decided to start our day early and photograph various holiday celebrations throughout the region. We make the command decision to begin at the Veterans' Cemetery, which embroiders the hillsides and flatlands on the north side of Santa Fe with row upon agonizing row of headstones commemorating among them the many who have given their lives that we might live.

I'm itchy to begin, for, at long last, I've commandeered a new Leica camera with its razor sharp 35 mm f2 lens. For the longest time I've wanted to be able to get close to people, up in their face so to speak, without being too intrusive like what can happen with a much larger, much noisier, camera. The Leica meets those specifications exceptionally well: a shutter so quiet, a hummingbird can drown it out merely by flying by during its discharge. And the camera itself, unless one recognizes the makes of cameras easily, looks almost like a toy: the inexpensive, five and dime store variety. But it feels good, really good, in my hands: enough heft to know you have command of the body, and the bright frame outline in the viewfinder places me in full control of what's to be in each image, with the benefit of knowing who or what's about to come into its outer edges.

After an early morning rich, aromatic coffee and delectable scone at a favorite, Sage Bakery, we head to the cemetery and immediately run into a traffic jam. I had no idea it would be this crowded so early. Parking spaces are hard to come by, but with some skillful scouting we land at one no one else would dare try to fit in. Siegfried escapes the passenger's seat in favor of playing traffic cop and with every bit of training I received while learning to drive in New York we safely nestle graveside.

Before I go on, I'd like to tell you about how Siegfried and I first met. It's an important foundation for the rest of this story.

I had traveled to Santa Fe to housesit for a week and brought with me an older 5X7 film camera I had just recently come upon. I wanted to see if I could get the lens calibrated before I did a test run with it. I stopped in the camera shop and asked if the lens could be calibrated in the next couple days, so I could try it out before returning home. "No, I couldn't do that, I'm tied up for a couple weeks with work as it is," the attendant responded.

The next moment I heard a male voice ask the attendant, "Why don't you loan him one, so he can at least try out the camera?"

"I don't have one that will work for him," came the response.

"Well, I do. Why don't you come over to my house for a cup of coffee in the morning? I have a 10 AM appointment, but we could at least chat a bit before that. Let's say 8 o'clock. By the way, my name is Siegfried Halus, pleased to meet you."

"Thank you for your generous offer, Siegfried. I'm Jim Young. Let me have your address and I'll see you in the morning."

Long story, short, I showed up promptly at 8 and Siegfried had both coffee and breakfast prepared. At that moment, I knew, without question, that we were destined to be lifelong friends. He asked me about the camera and we spoke about photography for a while. Siegfried was a world-renowned photographer who taught locally and it was a wonderfully wandering conversation about things important to both of us.

In short order, Siegfried told me of his recent divorce and related happenings, which obviously touched him deeply. I joined him on his canvas of life, as I had also been recently divorced and had similar feelings. We shared much, exhibited deep compassion for one another, shed tears together.

As our chat began to wind down, he realized it was beyond 10 AM and he had missed his previous appointment. He dismissed it out of hand, saying: "Nothing could be so important as having just met a good friend." We embraced, committed to visit again before I left town, and went on our separate ways—yet deeply connected.

That's the character of my friend, Siegfried. And we remained close friends until his untimely demise just several years ago. I miss him still—and always will. There are many more stories to tell, all of which made us both richer by the living of them.

Now to return to the original intent of this story.

Siegfried and I trade glances as we begin to engage with the surrounding environment. I snap an unusual angle of rows of American flags blowing their salutes to the mysterious heroes and heroines who lie beneath our feet. I feel like I've just entered the mouth of a maze that goes nowhere and everywhere at the same time, out into eternity.

Siegfried loads his medium format camera, plus his 35 mm, so he can cover any shot he wants, in any way he wants. I focus my attention on the feelings that are beginning to well up from deep inside, stirred by the blend of music playing in the background—a ballad here, a military march there—each working its way into my psyche.

I sense that today will be a day of deep connections, even though I never had engaged in military duty myself, except for ROTC in my first year of college. Actually, that was the highest grade I got that first semester. On second thought, perhaps I've missed my real calling.

Siegfried and I agree to split and each go our own way, beckoned by whatever pulls us, one way or the other. I find myself drawn to a family of Hispanic men, women and children. They are gathered on lawn chairs, blankets, with some meandering to and fro, depending upon what draws their attention. I ask if they mind if I photograph them and almost in unison they gleefully grant permission. As I focus, one of the family, a young woman, decides to sit down in the chair behind her. Her decision throws the photo out of the natural arrangement that made it so special, so I beckon her to stay standing and suggest to all of them that they just continue going about their business.

They show their command of the situation by posing instead, each one in her or his own private majesty. It is then that I notice that one of them, a man in his middle twenties I'd say, is obviously physically challenged. Yet, it is just as obvious that, to this family, he fits in beautifully as part of a larger glow to which he contributes. "No judgmental nature here," I think to myself. I snap one; then another; and then a last one, saying, "Now, at least, pretend that you like each other." They break into a wildly laughing portrait and paint the horizon with sheer joy over the idea—fully catching the intended irony of my admonition. I thank them once again and move on, creating various compositions, mostly of family and individuals that attract me, for one reason or another. Each time I feel a special connection with those collaborating with me today. Each time my soul seems to light up with a deep inner glow.

Something in the periphery to the left attracts me: a band of soldiers dressed in uniforms of a bygone era. The group, eight or nine in number, is composed of a few Hispanics, but mostly African Americans, representing the Black Brigade that served in New Mexico some generations earlier. I saunter over to the group and chat with them a bit, ending my conversation by asking if I could photograph them. They gift me with a lovely array of photos, some informal, some very formal, along with some close-ups of their age-worn weapons, somewhat ill-fitting uniforms, and dusty boots. I take leave with a heart filled with gratitude for the experience, but even more important, for the service they and their predecessors have given to our country.

I meander a bit, and rest to sip some badly needed water so I don't get dehydrated. As I rest under the crown of a broad shade tree, I catch the eye of an elderly gentleman adorned in a uniform from what looks like WW II. He salutes me from across the way. I salute him back and edge through the crowd to introduce myself to him. He proudly lifts his discharge papers from his inside breast pocket and unfolds them so I can see who had signed them. Elegantly he presents himself as an officer who had been discharged by none other than President Dwight D. Eisenhower. It's almost as though he is the only one to have achieved this good fortune. At least in his mind that appears so. There couldn't be a man more proud than Clyde is, and he beams that pride as I photograph him in majestic salute, shoulders back as through holding a rolled towel between his shoulder blades, face furrowed with wisdom's lines, tummy tucked in to hide the chest somewhat fallen by age. Elegant. He is simply elegant. In a snap, Clyde spins abruptly to salute a comrade from another era—and I permanently etch their intimate connection on the film that lines my heart; an indelible imprint that will forever enrich my soul.

A few speakers introduce still others. and remarks seemingly drone on in the midmorning heat that is building. At one point the Black Brigade is introduced and marches dutifully forward to present the colors to the gathering. I notice yet another elderly gentleman nearby, also proudly dressed in uniform of another era, showing respect by his perfectly executed salute. I edge over to create an image through the opening of his salute, holding the flags drifting in the breeze beyond in focus: a stunning image of real patriotism if I ever saw one. I wait patiently when the ceremonies break for a few moments and nestle up to this marvelously tailored gentleman as he initiates a conversation with a much younger Hispanic man, obviously a Green Beret from a bygone era himself. It was an exquisite juxtaposition of the young and the old, Hispanic and Gringo, the stout and strong and the thin and frail, yet obviously equally proud and glad to have served their country.

After chatting for a bit to learn more about them, I ask permission to photograph them and they provide me with what they thought I wanted: eyes straight on, bodies stiff at attention, chins pulled into their chests, tummies tight, buttocks tucked. I ask if they might face and salute one another and they gratefully oblige. In doing so, the elderly man catches Clyde's image nearby and turns to salute him as well. What extraordinary images these are, captured both on film and as well on the lining of my heart.

By this time I sense that I was about out of film on this roll and check the counter on top of the camera. I don't have my glasses on, but it looks like the roll might be finished, so I cock the shutter to see if this is so. It cocks as though there is more film to use, but something inside me says to check it out. I can feel my stomach beginning to rumble in anticipated distress. I take out my reading glasses and, to my surprise, the counter reads 38. My stomach now lurches at the prospect of not having seated the film properly. I feel a self-inflicted tirade coming my way. I slowly walk to the shade and gently open the camera back just a speck so as not to ruin more than a few shots if the film still has some room for creation.

My worst fear is realized, as the roll of film is still entirely in the starting position. Not a single image that has lined my heart has been recorded on film. I throw some kerosene on the now huge flaming self-castigation, calling myself every name in the book, including expletives that ought to know better. Yet, in an instant, I feel something within bump me hard: the recognition that a more important lesson has arrived to take me to a higher level of spiritual consciousness.

There I stand, filled with upset over the fact that I hadn't been careful enough to thread the film properly in the seemingly difficult receptacle; upset that my fear of such a thing happening actually generated the result of the feared end. The real lesson appears hot on the heals of the first, that which was only an illusion, and I find myself quickly abandoning the huge load of self-judgment I am inflicting. The real lesson becomes abundantly clear: it really isn't the images captured that make for success. It's only the exchange of loving life energy that has been allowed to brighten another's day that really matters. On that scale of expression, it has been a perfect day. In that very instant, I can feel a quelling of the internal fire that was destined to burn me to a crisp, quenched now by the cool waters of a much deeper knowing of Truth for me.

With that behind me, I load the camera as Siegfried rejoins me for the next leg of our Memorial journey. Setting out for Taos via the High Road, we stop briefly at a corner lot filled with a display of rugs. Siegfried photographs them from front and rear, while I photograph the children playing nearby as they occupy time with self-designed games. It's amazing what fun people can have simply by inventing ways to do so along life's byways.

Lazily, we head into the noon day sun and decide to meander off the main road to inspect several sparsely populated gatherings along some back roads of northern New Mexico. We stop at one point to rinse our sweaty faces with the cool spring waters and sit back to admire the braces of wildflowers that paint the banks of the stream and beyond. It is a glorious day in northern New Mexico, with brilliant azure skies lit by electric white clouds floating like giant cotton balls in the gentle breeze. We are taken by the sight and for a time succumb to its power to nourish. Silently, we simultaneously head toward the car, creating a few images along the way.

Siegfried cusses as he inspects his medium format camera. "What's up?" I ask. "Oh, I forgot to adjust the f-stop and didn't get what I wanted out of that last shot or two." "No biggie," I respond, with my own earlier episode still foremost in my mind, "it's just a photo or two." Siegfried moans a few epithets at himself and I laugh, now knowing how utterly silly it is to bemoan a simple mistake that can inform one of the need for higher consciousness.

We fold back into mutual silent reflection, and almost absent-mindedly head through Chimayo. Its provocative presence suddenly jars us with its beckoning, a beckoning to photograph at the Santuario there. I create some of what feel like all-too familiar images, but I never tire of being in that space and collaborating with this person or that object. Today is no exception. After a few moments, feelings of hunger prove to be stronger than the urge to create, so we adjourn for the time being to indulge ourselves with a luscious late lunch at the Rancho de Chimayo.

The warm sun embraces us as we dine outside, filling our bellies with scrumptious, authentic Mexican cuisine and a welcome, medium-sized, ice cold pitcher of frozen margaritas. We're both in a mood for a nap as a result of the overriding effect of the events of the day, combined with the nourishment that has refreshed our physical being and the imagery that has nourished our souls.

Panza allende y corozon contento—a full stomach and a contented heart—a fitting expression for what has turned into two sleepy amigos now occupying lounge chairs in the shade as a respite before continuing to Taos through Truchas, a small, mostly Hispanic village, a few miles and several planting zones higher beyond. Siegfried and I seem to be in full synchronicity today, as we pull ourselves out of our New Mexico Lazyboy chairs and head for the car. Slowly we climb the hillside roads into Truchas, where we find not a community celebration, but a sprinkling of families decorating and tidying up several gravesites. The first is one containing a brace of motorcycle replicas adorning adjoining gravesites. A middle-aged couple works in tandem, tugging at weeds, exploring the soil, and planting new, bright plastic flowers in the urns provided.

We strike up a conversation and learn that they are from Albuquerque, but have lived in Truchas before, and intend to return again, soon. They make it clear that these are the gravesites of their niece and her boyfriend who were killed in a motorcycle accident a few years before. The still are uncomfortable talking about it, yet gladly oblige our request to photograph them exercising their self-appointed chores. Siegfried wanders away, but I stay in place, photographing some, conversing some, all the while feeling the residual pain of these new acquaintances. These are special moments. They remind me of the earlier lesson prompted by the improper threading of film, and my heart melts even further to the cause of relationship. We are lent to each other this way, it seems to me.

We head towards Taos, with Siegfried driving this time. We stop at a few galleries along the way, seemingly satisfied with our day's "take," but perhaps for different reasons. As we pull up the last mountain pass before entering Taos, I glance at my camera and am inspired to check my film count once again. I interrupt the warm spring air with a burst of uproarious laughter, blurting out, "Okay, OKAY! I get it! I GET IT!" Siegfried turns with a start: "What the hell's going on with you?" he inquires.

"I did it again."

"You did what again?"

"I loaded the film incorrectly and didn't capture a single image I've created today."

"You've got to be kidding!"

"Nope, now you know why I said not to be so disturbed at losing just an image or two down in Chimayo. I didn't get a single one all day! But you know what, Siegfried? I've learned—or relearned yet again—a much more valuable thing than being careful about how I load the film."

"What's that?" he rejoined.

"It's the truth about the creative act. The process is more, much more, than merely a vehicle to get to some product. And in this case, the photographs are not really the products to be savored. The real product is the profound life episode that quickens and forever enriches the soul, creating an indelible print on the lining of my heart. In this way of thinking the process and the product become one in the same—and life is validated as the gift it itself is."

No response, except the wisdom found in silent self-reflection. Simultaneously we are enfolded in a state of grace. In a moment's time, we simply catch one another's eye and a knowing smile adorns both of our faces in the satisfaction of sacred truth having permeated our being. My camera stays in its carrying case the rest of the day as I savor the marvelous gifts of life I have been blessed with this day, especially the gift of being able to travel along life's ways with my lifelong friend, Siegfried.

Truly, it *is* Memorial Day.

HOW COULD I?

I have come to view the number 13 as a sacred number, particularly because of its representation of Jesus and the twelve disciples, and because of its designation in I Corinthians: 13, the verse describing perfect (whole) love.

With this story, there is even more reason to view it as sacred. It begins on the evening of Friday the 13th of January, 1995. I, among 38 other men and women from all walks of life, am in the midst of a month-long program to become a spiritual director, held at the Pecos Benedictine Monastery in Pecos, NM. It is about 9:45 in the evening, at the end of a long and fruitful day. Just moments before, I had decided to stay on in the lounge for a bit longer, chatting with several classmates while peeling an orange.

In walks Rachel, carrying a folded piece of paper, obviously on a mission. She comes directly to me, hands me a "note" in outstretched hand and says, "Here, I've been told to give this to you." "Who's it from?" I inquire. "I've just been told to give it to you." "Does it need an answer?" "Nope!" And she disappears, just as unexpectedly as she had appeared.

I open the note and am deeply moved by its contents, but can't immediately figure out why Rachel has given it to me. So I refold it, finish chatting with friends and head off to bed. Just before retiring for the night, I reread the note, searching for the connection. Here is what the note said:

"1/13/95 for Jeffrey Martin Magoon
      Born July 8, 1959
      Died in a fire July 26, 1965

"Small angel son, I sensed your presence with me as I sat before the Blessed Sacrament tonight. I heard the soft rustle of wings and felt the gentle touch of a kiss upon my cheek. Tonight I heard your voice say: 'Mama, it's me, Jeff. Abba wanted to send an angel to you to fill your heart with peace and reassure you of His love, and I asked If I could come along.'

"Silent tears have streaked my cheeks and quiet gratitude has filled heart. How I have missed you, my precious one! The raw, gaping wound so brutally opened by your parting has long since closed. Only the scar remains. The gift of healing and the grace of acceptance have been given. But the missing doesn't go away, nor does the special love my heart holds for you and you alone, my firstborn child.

"What a thoughtful and loving gift—that you have been sent to bring me deeper knowledge of our Father's love. I will not try to hold or capture you. I sense that if I were not able to let you go then one other than you would have been sent to do the Father's will. I am so grateful for this loving gift and I praise and thank Abba, Father, Brother Jesus, and dear comforting Friend, Spirit, for granting your request.

"Stay close, little one, for as long as you are permitted, and though my love for you cannot compare to the love you now enjoy, please know dear son that my heart sings a gentle lullaby of love to you each time I sense your presence and a glorious hymn of praise to the One who loved us both into being--the One who now sustains me through each moment of my life."

I am touched even deeper at this reading, feeling the pain of my friend Rachel beyond belief, but I still can't make the connection until, in a flash, I remember that my mother, too, had lost her first born, also James, of pneumonia, but a few days after he was born. I think and pray about the connection and go to sleep thinking that this "mystery" has been solved.

It's now the next morning and our classes focus on healing our inner child, using several nonverbal methods such as drawing, creating mandalas, writing poetry and the like. As Sister Geralyn makes her presentation, I quite effortlessly doodle and write brief phrases of verse. All the while, I can feel something deep inside me "moving," but can't figure out what is going on. I feel like something or someone else has control of my inner being. At the close of the hour, Sister tells us to take the next hour to create something we feel needs doing and return to share it with a small group as a way of honoring it. Seizing the moment, I exit directly to the chapel, feeling the need for a private, sacred place in which to create my "project."

Just as my back side hits the chair, I spontaneously break open like an egg, emitting uncontrollable sobs and agonizingly wailing: "Mom, oh, Mom, I'm so sorry for your pain! I'm so sorry for your pain!" Over and over again; over and over. I could not have imagined such pain and sorrow. Just then several unexpected guests come into the chapel, so I remove myself to a small counseling room off the entry to the chapel. Again, as I hit the chair, I break open, repeating the crying out in pain, only this time even deeper and longer in duration. Although I know I am somehow feeling my mother's pain, I still don't know what is happening or why—until the verses that come through me begin to shape the story, and the drawing that follows reinforces its power of healing in me. The verse tells its own story:

How Could I?

Mom, oh, Mom
how could I ever have known
the depth of your pain
the breadth of your loss
from the death of your first born
James?
how could I ever have known?
how could I?

you never told me
in any way I could then recognize
the burden of such pain.
but now
with eyes anew
with vision of heart

I not only
know of your pain
I am at one
with your pain.

through the pain
of the mothers of lost children
God sent an angel and a child
Jeff, age six
to tell his mother
of God's Grace upon Jeff's soul
and hers;
with a message, too
for me.
I can hear James
but a few days old
calling to Jeff as he leaves:
"It's for Jim, too
for Jim, too!"

I didn't know, Mom.
how could I ever have known?
how could I!?
all the time I felt
deep within
you wanted me
perfect
when instead

you wanted me to just be
alive and safe from harm's way
free
from you fear of loss
and the pain loss renders.

how could I ever have known, Mom?
how could I?
but now
my inner Jimmy and I
both know
and in this single Loving stroke
of reaching from beyond
we all
are One at last
united in our pain, our love
and the understanding
that renders forgiveness unnecessary.

I love you, Mom; I love you, James;
I love you, Jimmy; I love you, Jim.
praise be to God
for the joy I now am.
how could I ever have known?
how could I?

My hands move quickly to create a drawing, as
though I have nothing to do with it, except to

hold the crayon. The imaginary hand only too dramatically depicts the intermingling of my mother's grief for the loss of James with my own development, and with that of my inner child. My mother is holding James and Jimmy in her arms, their figures intertwined. I am holding all of them in my loving caress. God holds us all in God's powerfully healing embrace. All are contained in what I at first felt was the red, egg-shaped seat of my emotions.

After soulfully sharing this dramatization with a few of my loving, compassionate classmates I go off to the men's room. As I open the door, I thank God for the beautiful image. As I do, immediately comes into view the large red ellipse, flashing like a neon sign, and I hear the word, WOMB, pierce my mind. In an instant I realize that I had picked up my mother's pain and grief while in her womb, and in that same instant I knew that any remnants of ill feeling toward my mother had completely disappeared. Talk about a miracle! And it was not yet over.

While sharing this story with my support group, one woman says that her mother had a miscarriage and she always wondered what affect it might have had on her. When I hand a copy of the verse to another, she weeps instantly in the recognition that she hadn't completed her grieving process over the loss of one of her children. Still another is affected similarly when Rachel shares the story with her group. And there is no way of knowing how many were touched but didn't—or weren't able to—say anything at all.

When Stella, one of our group, sees the date I had put on the verse (January 14, 1995), she says, "I don't normally pay any attention to dates on things, but do you know what January 14 is?" I allowed that I didn't, except that it was the day after Friday the 13th. She responds with, "Well, that's the date of the New Year in the Hellenic Orthodox Church." "What did you say?" I blurt out, astonished by her declaration. "It's the date of the New Year in the Hellenic Orthodox Church," Stella repeats. "I was baptized in the Greek Orthodox Church, Stella!" "Well, then, Happy New Year, Jim!" she cheers.

I share the entire story with Rachel later in the day, and she exclaims, "You don't know the half of it! I had an argument with God about giving you the note. God said to give a copy of what I had written in my journal to you and I said that I would feel foolish doing that. You wouldn't have any idea what it was about. God told me once again to do it. I argued once again, saying that you would think I was crazy. God again insisted. I worked out a deal with Him, saying that I would agree to take it down to the coffee lounge and if you were there I would give it to you, but if you weren't there, that would be a clear sign it wasn't for you."

I respond with my mouth gaping in astonishment, "Rachel, I was going to leave, but something told me I was supposed to stay a while longer, so I decided to have an orange." "I know," she says, with a wide smile on her lips and a knowing in her eye.

The story of what some would call this miracle of healing goes on and on as my spiritual director worked with me on its meaning in scripture over the next few weeks. It continues to this very day as other circumstances free yet more for healing, but you get the point. Giving our brokenness to the Universe results in an outpouring of love through many others in acts of immense proportions as they spread to all who are willing to accept the gift. So what formerly seemed to be miracles come to be everyday events, once we are open to them.

As it has been attributed to mystical Jesus, "And even greater works than these shall you do." Greater in this case perhaps meaning only more, for the acts are the same: acts of freedom, released by love, showing themselves as grace of the moment, the *real* miracle. Or perhaps greater simply because more people seem to be giving themselves to this labor of love, and over a longer time than Jesus was given in his human form. Loving is an exponential dimension, not just a numerical or geometric one. The more we give ourselves to love, the more love there is to give.

By our example, others are also freed to give.

And give they do.

YOU'RE MAYOR OF WHAT?

It's been more than two years since my wife left town. When I am tempted to offer an explanation for it, it is less painful to say that she left because she felt she simply couldn't live in any town that would have me as mayor—especially in a town called Deadmann Springs. It makes a good story line. And it's probably even at least partially true.

I've been called lots of things in my life, some good, some not so good, but—Mayor of Deadmann Springs? One friend even exaggerates the title by saying it in Spanish, making it sound exotic and grandiose all in one. C'mon, give me a break! How does someone get to be mayor of a place called Deadmann Springs, with the last official population declared at 111? Surely someone doesn't run for such a position. Why would anyone want to be a mayor in the first place?

Not that Deadmann Springs is a bad place to be mayor, if someone wanted to be one. Quite the contrary. It's a sweet, sleepy, bedroom community just north of Gingerhome, PA, which itself is known as Little Switzerland for the way its gingerbread homes are built on the sides of hills, attracting tourists galore for its vast array of simple and exotic arts and crafts. Add to that lots of good weather; good food, all the way from great burgers and BBQ to elegant and fine dining; a vast array of summer festivals like the Blues, Jazz and Classical music weekends; spiced by the likes of the PT Cruiser, VW, Corvette and Antique Auto rallies; and add to it what is probably the second largest number of wedding chapels in the world, where over a hundred weddings commit one to another on February 14th each year, the biggest business day of the year, and you have one fun place to live near. And if one suffers from all this goodness, they're enough massage therapists, healing waters, health store food, and healing elements to nourish both body and soul to recovery.

Deadmann Springs itself takes its name from one of the early settlers in this southwest region of PA, John I. Deadmann, who came here from Tennessee in about 1832. The ferry boat used to cross the Drygulch River near the present site of what is now the last of the one lane, wood plank, expansion bridges in the state. Swingman's Pass we call it, named after the hangman's nooses that used to swing from its underbelly. The town has a rich history, including a now defunct railroad that once ran through town, connecting us with Gingerhome. And the once rumored story that Deadmann Springs was a bedroom community for Gingerhome in more ways than one still makes for occasional idle curiosity. To be honest, it's not really so occasional and surely not so idle.

The truth of the matter is that in many ways Deadmann Springs has the best of all worlds. It sits at the mouth of old Drygulch as it empties into Emptymouth Lake, so canoeing and other boating are celebrated in fine style without being intrusive. There is excellent fishing in and around Deadmann Springs for both bass and trout enthusiasts. Ordinances allow for in-home businesses, although from the looks of things, one would never know any businesses existed at all. The natural beauty of the town's forests along the riverside walking trail and in the picturesque RV park nourish resplendent. The recent establishment of a wildlife trail along the riverfront, intended primarily to encourage butterfly inhabitation, is becoming a paradise for various forms of other wildlife. We have our very own B & B, the Deadmann Springs Inn, which proudly fashions a baker's dozen lovely, antique-filled guest rooms, with scrumptious breakfast and cozy late afternoon wine and hors d'oeuvres. And just to spice life up a bit, several times a year folks from in and around town engage one another in the joy-filled, musically rendered atmosphere of a good, old-fashioned hootenanny at the town community center; great food, exuberant singing, inspired line-dancing and all. Couple that with a blue heron rookery of over forty nests nestled high in the trees that grace a branch of a full flowing river, a recent sighting of no less than eight bald eagles standing at attention not fifty yards from where I sit, and a few beaver dams punctuated by the slapping of a flat, broad tail on water that sounds more like the crack of a 30-30 rifle, and you have some breathtaking views of a treasured life.

And the citizens of Deadmann Springs, what about them? Well, they're mighty friendly when they want to be, not so much so when they don't want to be, just like folks most everywhere I've lived. A case in point is that you could go days, sometimes weeks, unless you have a post office box, that is, and then it's impossible, but you could go a long time without seeing or being troubled by anyone in town.

Yet, on this Thanksgiving, less that a week away, our second annual holiday dinner is being held in the community center. Last year when we initiated it some were skeptical, but still about thirty folks attended. This year the attendance is reaching into the mid-forties and still counting. Scrumptious turkey, stuffing, hot rolls, mashed potatoes and gravy, and drinks are provided, and the price of admission is simply a dish each of your favorite vegetable and dessert to be shared with the rest: food truly fit for a king and queen.

We've got plenty of characters who reside here, with four actual mayors in town, three ex- and one current, plus at least a cadre of folks who think they ought to be. A grand bunch of folks overall, mostly middle aged and beyond, with a healthy sprinkling of younger folks who will surely add to the richness of this delightful place called home. Sounds like a great place to live—and it is. It also sounds like I'm either the mayor or the president of the local chamber of commerce, but we don't have the latter, and probable never will, so that doesn't count.

How'd I get to be mayor? That's a long story. I'll make it short—well, shorter. The shortest version is the truth: no one else wanted it. Months before I was tapped for this dubious distinction I had been asked to be on the Zoning and Planning Commission. I had done such things before in a previous incarnation in western New York, so agreed to serve. Before I knew it, I was elected chairman of the group, and we embarked on a revision of our Town ordinances, primarily to update them to be in line with more recent State statues, and to avoid future difficulties on zoning matters. We became involved in an extensive rewriting which included not only our original intention, but the establishment of policies that would keep the town pretty much as it is, including limiting animals like pigs, chickens, emus, llamas and cattle from being raised for profit.

At the time, our commission consisted of a retired gentleman, let's call him Don, who has very strong opinions and a sense that only everything done in the past is reverent and therefore irrevocable; a very bright, highly experienced, outspoken and strong woman, let's call her Sarah—well, you get the point, got to protect the innocent and not so innocent, all in one—anyhow, who has had considerable experience of this kind in a larger metropolitan area; a cheerful yet pragmatic woman, Susie, who makes absolutely the very best sticky buns in the world, doesn't mince words, and who has the best interests of the town at heart; Mac, a young man with a degree in public policy who is bright as the day is long and right-minded, even if a bit naive in matters politic—things of a political nature turn his stomach, actually; Alfred, our town attorney, who's a stickler for the law and an extremely knowledgeable, extremely competent, extremely funny guy, who just happens to be my landlord's son, and the one who I let convince me to stay in town despite my divorce. All in all, these folks were doing a superb job rewriting the ordinances.

One of the many pluses for me was to have the benefit of being able to watch the personalities unfold during our deliberations. The most profound, simply because it seems to parallel the general character of mainstream America, occasioned the sparks that sometimes flew between our frequently protective retiree, Don, and our strong, bright, and forthright woman, Sarah. Many men who view themselves as strong simply cannot abide women who are strong, perhaps even stronger than they are. It's a sad fact, but very evident in day-to-day affairs of state, even today in our neighborhoods and homes. It's probably the very reason why Hillary will have an enormously difficult time becoming President, although no one, except in Florida that is, knows how people will vote once in the booth.

Back to the story. An opening became available on the City Council (can you imagine a town of 111 people having a "city" council?), and I was asked to fill it. I accepted, but felt somewhat guilty about leaving behind what was becoming an ever-growing amount of work by the Zoning and Planning Commission. In the end I thought I could still support the work by being their "patron saint" on the Council. Strange, how we can justify most anything.

In early spring a few years ago, I ventured to New Mexico as I fairly frequently do, to house-sit a home for some friends there. When I returned I found that our then mayor, Joe, had resigned due to the fact that he had undertaken several operations over just a few months and needed time and less stress to assist in his healing. Josie, our Recorder/treasurer, was the "interim mayor" by statute and called our group together for the purpose of selecting a mayor to fulfill Joe's term. Joe had been a strong mayor, with lots of administrative experience, so would be difficult to replace. But then, each of the current aldermen could certainly bring her or his own attributes to the cause if chosen.

The election could hardly be called that. Josie called the meeting to order and declared the purpose of the meeting. Several chimed in that it would be good if Josie just continued on with the job until the next election, but she allowed that she had a young child to raise and just couldn't see herself doing that, too. Then, one by one, each of the aldermen found a way to obviate the necessity for them to serve. As I heard each explanation as to why this or that one couldn't be mayor, I thought that my reason for not being named was as good as any of theirs, and prepared myself to vote someone else into the mayors position for the betterment of all. When it came my turn I simply declined because my house was for sale and said that I could well be leaving the community in a month or two. "Well," said one of the members, one obviously far more clever than I am, "if you did leave that soon, we wouldn't be any worse off then than we are now, so why don't your take it? With your background, it would be a breeze." I was moved to uproarious laughter by his take on the issue, and before I could gather myself and launch my own defense the rest fell in behind his line of thinking. They had dodged the bullet and it ricocheted off the exit sign and struck me right in the behind. In a flicker of a moment I had been snookered into being the next Mayor of Deadmann Springs. That simple: railroaded into a job that could someday just get me railed out of town.

The next morning, while fetching my mail from the post office, our Postmaster (she prefers to be called postmaster instead of postmistress because the term postmaster has more power in it) congratulates me and says, "Gee, Jim, won't that look great on your resume?" "Oh, goodness," I thought, "don't tell me I've worked in leadership positions most of my adult life only to have being Mayor of Deadmann Springs on my resume. Surely this couldn't be true!" Here I am, true or not.

I must drift a moment and say this about the very best postmaster in the universe. She provides the widest array of services in the nation, from properly dispensing news and messages both good and bad, housing articles and other information about our beloved town, displaying artistic renderings by local citizens of our famous Swingman's Pass, caring for the garden in front of the post office and our sign welcoming people into the world of nostalgia, and providing an herb garden for all to nourish their summer fare with. All this, on top of prompt, full service from the US postal service, each day delivered with a cheerful, uplifting attitude. She's far better than the best apple: a visit a day with her keeps the doctor away for most of us, that's for sure!

Well, since that first appointment there's been another election where the aldermen and recorder/treasurer ran for two-year terms and I for the official four. I pride myself, actually the council and recorder/treasurer, too, on being elected unanimously in that election of 2002.

And not one of us, as far as I know, spent even a single penny on the campaigns for reelection. What a model to be replicated on the state and national level! Well, the truth is that we all ran unopposed. But it's still also true that not a single vote was cast against any of us. How many people can make that claim—on any level?

What's it like being Mayor of Deadmann Springs? Like most everywhere else, I suppose. Can't do much right, lots wrong, as least to some people. Fact is, though, most people are so involved in their own lives that they're oblivious to what's going on around them. Besides, I face this marvelously fun-filled challenge with a somewhat different attitude. As long as I continue to find the fun in it, and we're doing some good, I'll continue.

Plus I learned long ago that it's none of my business what anyone else thinks about me, or what I do and don't do. They're entitled to their opinion and I'm entitled to mine, and I don't take anyone else's personally. Doing such a foolish thing could only get us all into trouble.

In this matter, I'm reminded of a favorite poem of mine by Persian poet Hafiz, in which he tells what happens when egos get in the way, if I may paraphrase: the thought that one man is either better or worse than another quickly breaks the wine glass. Indeed, when we place either ourselves or another on a pedestal, we are quick to fall from the grace that permits unfettered harmony among and between peoples. It's a lesson we might learn and learn well, lest we demean the sacredness of human dignity more than we already have in this world.

As time passes, I am coming to both know and appreciate this lovely town more and more. People have become more than mere faces to me. Their character comes into full bloom as I get to know them better. More and more I see them as simply good people, informed by their history, moved to speak on behalf of that history, something I have always admired and respected—and something I believe we ought to honor as we traverse this planet. After all, it's the shoulders of all those that come before us that we stand on. It's their labors of love that have paved the way, provided the foundation for our very own. Their sacred stones comprise the very foundation upon which we continue to build. Thank God for every bit of it—and all of them!

You can believe me when I say this mayor thing has been fun-filled. How so? Well, just having the opportunity to guide people through thorny issues and some not so thorny, but that which appear so to some, is fun. It's reframing the issues and concerns that makes it fun; helping folks see something in a new light, at least perhaps for them. It's dealing with all kinds of personalities, yet seeing beyond personality to the innate goodness within all, so each has her or his dignity maintained, no matter what the position taken, even how it's taken. It's offering up ideas for enriching our community, and watching some take and others fade, even go up in a blaze of glory, and still coming back with more. It's encouraging others to do likewise, that each may have the opportunity to contribute. And it's always, and I do mean always, honoring those that have come before us, upon whose shoulders we stand. It's just being an example for some of this that's the most fun, for to do so is just my own personality showing its way, just one among all the others. No better, no worse, just different.

It's also working side-by-side planting bulbs so the wildlife trail will be a haven for butterflies and hummingbirds and other festive wildlife. It's tapping into one of the State engineer's love for Swingman's Pass and letting him talk me through the process of how he's going to renovate the bridge and then talking him into painting it the original golden color instead of a nondescript silvery nothingness. It's about keeping townsfolk informed via a periodic newsletter called the *THE DEADMANN SPEAKS,* and getting donations for our wildlife trail and the foundation stone that will house the plaque commemorating that space for the now defunct, but nonetheless hugely contributory, Deadmann Springs Fire Department Women's Auxiliary. It's having our first Community Appreciation Day where we honored everyone in the community for their contributions, and celebrating our very first Arbor Day, planting two pink dogwoods in memory of a dear resident couple who passed on last winter.

Yes, it's even having a ribbon-cutting ceremony for our septic tank, our new privies and shower stalls that now bless our RV park after some twenty years of the community holding that vision. It's even publicly noticing that one of our town folks, a lovely, sweet woman, who just happens to be my landlady, is the granddaughter of one of the founders of Arbor Day, and watching her bathe in the simple recognition that lights her spirit. And, of course, it's fun simply learning and growing in character from it all.

When I think of all these joy-filled receptacles, I'm caused to wonder if this mayor thing isn't serving in some ways as the replacement love of my life, allowing me to continue exercising the loving attitude that emits joy from the creative act of authentic relationship. On a time and task level I don't feel I'm married to being mayor. That is, I'm not driven by it to the exclusion of other people and things that are important to me. Yet, upon serious reflection I find that it does provide me with genuine opportunities to give without expectation of results or return, something the truth about loving expresses in genuine relationships of any kind, let alone marriage. I'll have to let this idea perk some more and wait for wisdom to reveal the truth.

Regardless, it's fun just being able to celebrate life for the gift it is, and to honor and validate the richness of life that can be found in everyone and every thing. My father, the best man I've ever met, taught me how to do that, how to find joy in all I do. And I stand here today as but a simple human being, grateful in every way for being honored with the privilege of this extraordinary gift.

Any downsides to report? Perhaps, but not the ones you'd normally think of. What to some might be considered troublesome phone calls for help on one matter or another, and being asked to settle what are mostly petty differences, just come with the territory and further the development of mediation skills. What really bothers me are those times when people can't see past their immediate convenience or beyond the end of their noses to the attendant good for their children or grandchildren. Take, for example, our major project to obtain city water for all, which, despite over five years of hard work by many, plus a town referendum, failed to come to fruition because almost half of the folks wouldn't trust enough to sign the appropriate documents that would permit state funding.

And then there's the dog—or better named—the leash ordinance. It seems like those whose animals are the biggest offenders are those most opposed. Isn't that the way? We're far from being at the dog pack stage, but a few of us want to head that off before it occurs. It doesn't take much to tip the scales. In just the last few months we've had two people nipped or bitten and one fall to a broken arm, and a few who walk for exercise scared nearly out of their wits, just because people won't take responsibility for their pets. Well, we're headed for a showdown in the next meeting or two. At the last council meeting I let it be known that I'd be stepping up to the bully pulpit soon, and gave them a little sampling. "Just last week we had a young couple and their nine year old son move in, and when I went over to welcome them to town the gentleman said to me: 'Mr. Mayor, I hope you don't think us inhospitable, but the first thing I told our neighbors is that we're building a fence around our back yard so our dogs won't be bothering anyone around town.' "Now, that's music to my ears, someone, especially as young as they are, taking responsibility for their animals. And then, there's a member of this very council" I continued, "who, when his dog simply nipped someone who fussed at her, had her put down. Can you imagine a feeling that strong about accountability? Well, that's what I can only commend people for, and what I'm going to be looking to you, this town's leadership, to provide when this item comes off the table at the next meeting." Will it work? I don't have the vaguest notion. What I do know is that we must try to do the best for the greater good, or get out of the business, out of town—or both.

There is one thing I do miss, though. Before our beloved bridge was completely renovated last year, it played like a fine-tuned instrument in the New York Philharmonic—well, okay—more like a hootenanny band in the 80's, 1880's that is: thumpety thump thump, thumpety thump thump, CLANG; thumpety thump thump, thumpety thump thump, thumpety thump thump, CLANG, it went, like the angelic gifts that put one's heart back in rhythm in the dark of night. Now, with a new face along with the huge timber replacements interlaced, it plays more like a washboard and thimble solo without accompaniment. I guess this is just Nature's latest way of planting nostalgia in the souls of our citizens. But I do miss the original sonata just the same.

Nevertheless, on balance, I consider myself a very fortunate man to be Mayor of Deadmann Springs, PA. Indeed I am. What transpires between and among the people is energizing, sometimes momentarily debilitating or at least somewhat disappointing, but energizing nevertheless. It inspires me to be only what I can, no matter what the condition, no matter what the circumstance. My life is enriched beyond measure to be able to see into the heart of each individual and, in the final analysis, do what I can to honor that heart space while still doing my very best to keep a handle on the action that could hopefully be in the best long term interest of all concerned. A challenge? Oh, sure. Fun? You bet! Let me provide one last example to illustrate what I mean by fun.

Just the other day I presented an idea to the City Council. A few days earlier at the post office I had forewarned one of the aldermen about the idea, hoping that by giving him a "heads up" on it that he would find a way to help me obtain approval. Not really. I just planted it to see how much fun we could have with it. Here's the idea as I presented it to the council:

"RECOMMENDATION TO THE DEADMANN SPRINGS CITY COUNCIL

"It is recommend to the Deadmann Springs City Council that we establish a replacement for the shoe tree that was disbanded in Gingerhome, and that once a year (at the end of the camping season) we have the fire department assist us in gathering the shoes from the tree, wash them, and send them to a charity for distribution to the needy somewhere around the world. By stressing the charitable nature of the project and suggesting that folks discard sneakers/athletic shoes in reusable condition rather than leather shoes, so it would be easier to cleanse and reuse them, we could collect something of value to redistribute. The benefits of such a project are manifold, some of which are: drawing attention to our community in a healthy way, while at the same time informing people about our RV park, nature trail and butterfly garden; renewing a sense of charity towards others; highlighting the necessity for a sense of humor and fun activities (of not taking ourselves too seriously); and providing us with the opportunity to work with the fire department for the good of others. All in all, this is an opportunity for uniting the community with a small, doable project that enriches the soul, both individually and collectively.

"The costs for this project are minimal, if any at all. It costs nothing for the tree, or for "relieving" the tree of its soles; the only cost would be to wash the athletic shoes and ship them. To defray costs and to perhaps add cash to the donation contributed, we could suggest that participants make a small donation to help defray such costs; such donation could simply be placed in the "after season" money slot at the RV park.

Suggested sign:

    "THE SOUL TREE
"This is the place where soles hang out,
the soles of you and me.
Yes, this is the place where soles hang out,
from souls that are fun and free.

"Welcome to "the town of friendly souls." This very special SOUL TREE was established as an opportunity for people to gather in fun to collect reusable sneakers/athletic shoes which can, on an annual basis, be distributed to those in greater need. We ask that you join us by also making a contribution of a $1 or so to help defray costs for cleansing and shipping this collection to the needy. Please do so in the donation box at the RV park entry booth. And by all means, enjoy your visit here! A map of our fair town, including references to our inventoried forest, nature trail, and butterfly garden are available at the RV park. THANK YOU FOR PARTICIPATING!"

Well, you can imagine my feigned chagrin when I asked the council for their comments. The first out of the bag was from the elderly gentleman I had been forewarned about, with his shoulders slumped and his head jutting out like a turtle from it's shell, as he shyly peaked out from under the frayed brim of his discolored baseball cap: "Nuh-uh, we sure don't need something like this in our town." And delivered with a smile at that! I could feel the rapidly growing uneasiness from the other council members, and the guests from the community that night seemed restless at best. I knew I was in for it on this one. All in the name of fun.

Next, the youngest member of the council spoke up, he, too, with a smile, the sort of smile that says, "I don't really like the idea, but nice try, Mayor," humoring me all along. He summarized what his look had already told me with, "I agree with Jobe—but I sure do like your poem."

The third in line didn't have to speak, although he's usually the one I can depend upon for a pragmatic, down to earth perspective to most anything we're discussing at the time. The look on his face said it all, as he lifted his eyes to meet mine, a look of utter disbelief forming his features, without words for others to hear: "Where the heck did you get this lame-brained idea?" (Actually, I think his look said something in language much stronger than this, but I need not report that here.) "You don't have to say anything, Carl," I responded, "you're look says it all," which diffused the tension some. A titter of laughter here and there began to set it free.

With one of the two women alderpersons absent, that left the last response to Darla, who is usually very thoughtful and intelligent about matters at hand. I could see that she didn't care much for the idea, but was fathoming the depths of her computer-like memory to come up with something to let me off easy; something rational, quite unlike how my proposal was envisioned. Time was pregnant with pause. After what seemed like an eternity I suggested, "That's okay, Darla, I think the rest of the group has rendered the proposal dead on arrival" "No, just a moment," she rejoined, "I'm just trying to recall...I think that the other one that was stopped was eliminated because someone had said that the shoes were responsible for killing the tree, and if we're applying to become a Tree City USA, that would be working against our purpose wouldn't it?"

I was about to respond with the fact that the shoes certainly couldn't kill a tree, especially because they'd only be there from April until October, but I suddenly realized that there was no turning this around, and decided to not prolong the agony. Darla's argument had settled it. Whether it was accurate or not, it gave the others what they needed to shift their energy to a silent, but nonetheless final, declaration expressed in their posture: "Whew, dodged another crazy idea from our mayor!"

All that was left for me to do, for my own sake as well as the sake of dignity for all, was to diffuse the situation with humor: "Well," I said with tongue in cheek, "if you're not going to support me on such monumental issues, I'm not sure you want me as mayor much longer." At last, some laughter to punctuate the relief. Surely, the proposal was as dead as a door nail.

On the way out the door that evening, the truth of it all became known. "You know, Jim," began one of the aldermen, "the people that the tree in Gingerhome attracted were nothing but drunks

and they caused all kinds of trouble there." I nodded a sign of understanding, but responded inwardly with a knowing smile, "I'm not a drunk—nor did I cause any trouble."
Well, that's okay, at least the seed has been planted. Maybe it'll take hold better in the warmth of the springtime sun as it brings up the flowers planted in our new butterfly garden last autumn. Everything has its own time and place.

Yes, I love being Mayor of this very special town called Deadmann Springs, and will remain so until I think it's time to move on.

Or until enough others think the same thing.

LIFE'S JUST FUNNY THAT WAY

Stage One

Last Christmas, right when we expected it least—but needed it most—life suddenly focused for us. Life's just funny that way.

We'd been living in Santa Fe, New Mexico for nearly four years, and although Helen Jane had learned to love the high dessert and its magnificent offerings, her soul began to stir—yearn, actually—for some "real dirt and real green trees," as she puts it. Having been born and raised in Arkansas, with plenty of both to ground her and hold the roots of her soul against the storms of life, she began to search for just the right mixture of these elements in Santa Fe and Taos. It wasn't too long before she declared her "real love" for nearby Taos, so we concentrated our energies on locating just the right place to tap our roots.

And search we did. We found one place on a little better than a half acre, a small stream meandering through one edge, including water rights. A treasure in that part of the world. But the house was very small and needed several tens of thousands of work to shape it to our personal specifications. In the midst of calculating how to make it happen, the owner accepted an offer higher than we could afford, so that one fell by the wayside.

Another reared its head, and although it seemed at first that it was what would satisfy, it ended up being barely that: a forcing of our desires on a space that really didn't meet the souls' needs. So, that one, too, fell. On and on and on it went.

We kept looking, but each time we found hope, the dwelling or the land (sometimes both) told us that this just wasn't for us. The heart didn't leap, the soul felt uneasy, peace was nowhere to be found. We'd just have to keep on searching for a new home we could embrace—one that would hug us back. Then came Christmas time with family in Little Rock; a time for sharing family values and precious time with special friends. And with it came hope.

Nearly a half-dozen times, both Helen Jane and I lost count, really, various friends and family offered—completely out of context with the conversation—something like the following. "Why don't you two move back to Arkansas? Not to Little Rock. Eureka Springs seems like just the right place for you." Each time it surfaced, of course, there were the usual denials, scores of reasons why returning to Arkansas wouldn't be the "right" thing for us to do. So we kept dismissing these callings out of hand.

On the way home in the car we chatted again about the number of times the suggestion had come up in conversation. And, again, we rejected it out of hand, but before doing so this time we allowed as such that Helen Jane had, on a number of occasions previously, mentioned her desire to live in closer proximity to her aging mother and aunts and uncles, now all in their mid-to-late 80's. In retrospect, I can see that the seeds of change had been planted and were beginning to take on the necessary water and light to nourish them. All they needed was a catalyst to give us a new view, a different perspective, without the self-imposed limitations that kept us from seeing our Truth.

After a long day's drive back to Santa Fe, we returned to our now-familiar surroundings. Greeting us when we opened the storm door to enter our condo was a package addressed to Helen Jane. As usual, we unpacked our belongings and sorted through the telephone messages and mail that had accumulated in our absence. The trip had taken its toll on us and we were about to take a nap to replenish our energy when I asked Helen Jane what the package was.

"Oh," she said, "I forgot to open it." Tiredly tearing through the outer wrapping, she found a card and gift, a belated birthday present from our younger daughter and her family in Oregon. After commenting on the sweet card, she exposed the gift from beneath the decorative wrapping: a cookbook written by Crescent Dragonwagon, a famous cook and author (and old acquaintance), formerly from—you guessed it—Eureka Springs!

Instantaneously, I commented: "What else needs to be said? What more prompting do we need before we give this idea of moving back to Arkansas consideration?" "Do you really think these are 'signs'?," asked Helen Jane. I knew to the depths of my soul they must be, and told her so. "Well," she conceded, "maybe we ought to look into this, after all."

By giving ourselves permission to begin looking at this new imagery, the strain of thinking about the possibility of such a transition went out of it. At least it did for me. It became clearer and clearer to me—deep down inside—that this was the direction we should be taking. Oh, we wondered how we'd do without our part-time jobs, both of which gave us great satisfaction and ample extra income. And the thought of leaving treasured friends pained us both. In the final analysis, though, although we knew we'd surely miss our friends, we knew we'd never forget them. We'd just carry them in our hearts wherever we went. Besides, we finally concluded, it will be fun introducing our old friends to new ones when they visited. Having decided to move forward—not without doubts, but in spite of them—all of them, and more new ones, soon began to fade as we undertook what has become yet another wonderful adventure together.

We began in earnest by asking people who ought to know about finding a trusted real estate salesperson in Eureka Springs. We came up with blanks until Kay, Helen Jane's sister, found the name of a fella named Doug from a friend of hers. "He owns a new hardware store in nearby Holiday Island, but my friend thinks he still sells real estate. He's supposed to be a real square shooter and honest as the day is long," she proffered. Over the ensuing weeks and months, we found her recommendation to be right on target. Doug was all that and more, and we took that as a good sign. Well, for the first trip and the three that followed HJ and I took turns at feeling the excitement about the possibilities—and then the disappointment that accompanied the failures to meet our dreams. One after the other, we were first encouraged by the descriptions of the possibilities for living, and their prices, only to find them lacking in one way or another. Not bad, mind you, just lacking in the basic elements we really wanted: not enough light; not enough usable space; not enough land; and little or no parking, despite the fact that the write-ups seemed to depict them otherwise.

Nevertheless, over the ensuing weeks we continued to step out in faith, searching for our new home and beginning to seek bids for moving and desirable mortgage interest rates. That may sound rather bold, but we had already put our condo up for sale without a realtor and, right at the end of our first weekend open house, a young man delighted in our place and made a full-price offer on it. Indeed, the wheels of progress seemed to be rolling along nicely.

Then one Friday, just as Helen Jane was about to visit her mother in Little Rock, we got a call from the young man purchaser in which he said his financing fell through. He was sorry, but we'd better move on and sell it to someone else, he

tells us. You can imagine our disappointment--
and our sudden burst of fear!! For a moment we
panicked, but in the context of loving, mutual
support, we quickly returned to our then-present
attitude: the overall picture is too large for us to
see, so just take everything in stride as being
what it's supposed to be. So, after agreeing that
we'd have another open house after Helen Jane
returned from her trip, she went on to visit her
mother. With that, our old confidence returned in
a flash.

Only to be dashed on Monday when I came home
from work. To my chagrin two new FOR SALE
signs greeted me as I pulled in the parking lot.
"How," I wondered, "will we ever sell ours now?
After all, our condo was larger than either of
those two, and the price was sure to be higher,
giving them the edge." I quickly decided to find
out the prices of the other two and, sure enough,
they were from 8 to 12 thousand dollars less
expensive. "But ours is SO SPECIAL!" I could
hear myself coaxing within.

That evening I told Helen Jane the news and she,
quite unexpectedly, readily dismissed my
concern. "Look, we sold it once, it will sell
again, only this time to the right person. And
don't worry about price, ours is priced right and it

won't have any difficulty selling." The rightness of her trust and faith cut to the quick and I immediately came to peace within. Trusting her good judgment and faith made it all the easier to feel my own.

Two days later, I returned home from work after lunch and saw three women in the parking lot, looking like they might be investigating the other two condos. Stepping out of the car, I asked if they were, in fact, about to do so, and they replied that they had just seen them, including another for sale by owner. Looking past the competition, I suggested that they'd be missing the best of the lot if they failed to look at ours. The realtor asked the woman from California who was seeking a new home, and her friend from Santa Fe, if they wanted to see ours as long as they were there. They quickly agreed and I suddenly realized that I couldn't remember in what condition I'd left our place that morning. Having made my disclaimer, that Helen Jane might be upset with me for showing the place without everything it is proper location, they laughingly agreed that it didn't really matter. And it didn't.

As they walked in the front door, I could sense their simultaneous gasp at the wonderful mid-day light filtering into the living space, the same light that had beckoned Helen Jane and me when we first experienced it. I watched the Californian closely as we went from one space to another: first into the open, cheerful kitchen; then out to the marvelously private, soon to be lush, garden patio; on to the upstairs bedrooms with private balconies outside each, overlooking the brilliantly-lit, snow-capped Sangre de Cristo Mountains in the distance.

As we entered the master bedroom, the Californian's friend asked, "Didn't you say your wife was away?"

"Yes," I responded, "why do you ask?"

"Well," said she as the other two entered the room, "I can't imagine my husband making the bed if I went out of town."

To which I responded amidst the laughter, "But what you don't know is that when Helen Jane's away I just turn back the corner of my side and slide in and out, so I don't have much bed to make that way."

That exchange seemed to break the ice and, shortly after, the potential buyer indicated that she had been looking for a condo for two weeks and was just about to give up when this "piece of paradise" showed up. "And do you know," she accentuated her proclamation, "when I lived in Santa Fe years ago I always dreamt of living somewhere on Agua Fria!" Before they left, she told me that I could expect an offer that afternoon.

Sure enough, I received a phone call from the realtor about half an hour later. "Will you pay us 3% for this qualified buyer," she inquired?

"No," I responded, "we'll sell it one way or another, so I'm not worried about it."

"Will you split the 3% with us?"

"No. And please don't bring anything less than a full-price offer, because it will only disappoint your buyer when we have to turn it down, and that wouldn't be fair to her."

"Okay, I'll be back to you."

Back she came: full-price offer—and a cash deal at that. Sticking to one's sense of what's right and fair does pay off.

So with the sale of our place out of the way,

Helen Jane went on to Eureka Springs from Little Rock and looked at more houses. Nothing came to the surface, so Helen Jane and I began to wonder if this "prophecy" of living in Eureka Springs wasn't also a closed door, like Santa Fe and Taos had turned out to be. We decided to return for one last try before giving up.

Meanwhile, Helen Jane continued her investigation for good moving companies and low mortgage rates. Quite to our dismay, both the moving costs and interest rates seemed to be escalating out of sight, giving us pause once again. But during a conversation with a friend, Helen Jane suddenly recalled the name of the mover who had relocated us to a Santa Fe suburb a few years ago; a likable chap with extraordinary care in moving and reasonable in cost, she remembered. She contacted him and, after evaluating our place for the move, he gave a bid that was a good bit less than the other three bidders. Talk about Grace!

Then, finding from our local finance person that the "going" mortgage rate was 7 1/8% plus a point—plus a half point to hold the rate for 30 days—HJ spoke with our Eureka Springs realtor and he recommended a few banks there. Helen Jane pursued them with a vengeance, and found that they were about the same as we'd been told locally. During our discussion of the topic, now again touched by fear, HJ had a sense that she should try the new bank in Eureka Springs called Community First Bank. "It just sounds right to me," she suggested. "With a name like Community First, how can it not be right for us?" I rejoined.

The next day Helen Jane contacted Community First and excitedly called me at work with the news. "Jim, can you imagine? They offered us a mortgage at 6.75%, with no points! Not only that, they'll hold that rate for up to 60 days without extra charge!" "Wow," I responded, "now if we only had a home to purchase." Life was getting funnier by the day.

At the beginning of the next week we traveled to Eureka Springs for our "last shot" at finding our dream home. We tagged it on to a trip to Tulsa, where my photo exhibit of the cloistered Carmelite nuns of Little Rock was accompanying the Tulsa Opera Company's performance of "Conversations on the Carmelites." By the time we saw our hosts on Friday evening yet another "miracle" had blessed us.

After several days of searching, now somewhat

frantically, about mid-morning on our last day in Eureka Springs our realtor suggested we take a ride into the country to see if some desirable farm land might be available. I looked at Helen Jane and she at me, both with eyes and souls seemingly vacuous by this time. "Okay," we said in unison, "but this is it for us." Doug admonished us not to be disappointed, that sooner or later something "just right" would surely show.

On the outskirts of Eureka Springs, we came to a decline that approached the White River, a wide body of water that connects Beaver Lake and Table Rock Lake. As we eased around the last curve before crossing, we were greeted by a miniature replica of the Golden Gate Bridge. Only this was a one-laner, with signs at both ends admonishing drivers to give way to approaching vehicles. The scene was as picturesque as any in a Vermont countryside view book.

Just as we left the bridge we saw a sign welcoming us to Beaver, AR, population 95; YOU HAVE JUST CROSSED THE BRIDGE INTO NOSTALGIA. BEAVER, ARKANSAS, A COMMUNITY OF NEIGHBORS. (Some people jokingly say nostalgia isn't what it used to be, but in Beaver it wonderfully is!) The sign was embraced by a large flower box filled with fresh spring blooms, no less. To say we were amused is an understatement.

We were further amused to see the general store and bed and breakfast off to the right on the roadway out of town. Just then something caught my eye: a blue and white house to the left on a knoll overlooking the bridge and river, with some kind of sign in front of it. I suggested we check it out and Doug swung the car over to the left and parked in front of what turned out to be a FOR SALE BY OWNER sign. Doug Doug went to the front door and spoke with the owner, returning with a broad smile on his face. "Well, she's headed to an appointment right now, but we'll get to see it at one o'clock this afternoon." Then he laughed. "What's so funny?" I asked. "She put the FOR SALE sign up just an hour ago!" Doug exclaimed.

That afternoon, we visited the house and spent nearly two hours going over it with a fine-toothed comb. We mused a bit, envisioned changes some, and left with a feeling that we might have just found our place. After all, it was a house with character, two bed rooms and two baths, 23 foot Pullman kitchen, warmly-lit sun room, cathedral-ceiling living room with an expansive view of the river, rock-walled room on the lower level with an entrance from outside, and a twenty-something foot elm tree growing seemingly from the center of the front deck—all on a half acre plus of land—and with a two-bedroom, two- bath guest house to boot.

We made an offer we could afford and it was turned down, primarily because the owner wanted a cash deal. Our realtor convinced the owner that we had excellent credit, punctuated by a promise of a letter of credit from a lender she would recognize and trust. We negotiated the selling price a bit over the weekend from our home in Santa Fe, and finally arrived at one that was fair to both the seller and us. Each gave a little, and the owners were extremely pleased to be able to keep their favorite bright crimson carpeting and complementary draperies.

Since then, I haven't slept much. Not out of any anxiety, but because my mind is running amok with ideas and visions for our new home. As I told Helen Jane, I haven't ever—not ever in the better than a dozen times I've moved in my adult life—been as excited about a move as I am this one. It just seems right for us to be closer to her mother and other aging relatives, as well as most of our siblings and in-laws. And the added benefit of living within an hour's drive of my exwife should give us the opportunity to see our sons and daughters and seven grandchildren more frequently. We've even found ourselves pointing out fun things to do with them already. The potential seems so powerful, and yet I can't fully explain it. All I know is that from time to time I feel waves of a peaceful love filling me to the brim, so much so that I can't seem to contain it. I don't think I'll spoil the feeling by over-intellectualizing it. My only prayer is that Helen Jane comes to be as excited about all this as I've become...I sense she is about to.

One thing for sure: not only had we learned that fear doesn't work, that only faith and trust does, but the rightness of this change in our lives has been affirmed in more ways than I can recall. It feels like we have indeed found a place we can embrace, and it seems to be hugging us back already. It's like the Universe has put out an all-points alert to help us know our Truth. Every single person we've talked to about this adventure we're on has, in one way or another, told us how fortunate we are: that Beaver is such a lovely place to live; that our neighbors are great—on and on. And with all the discussions about what changes we want to make in the house to make it our home, not once have we come close to becoming angry in disagreement. We just move on with a seemingly transcendent solution in hand.

As if that isn't enough, just this morning, as I was putting the finishing touches on this story, a female blue bird perched on the railing outside my window with a large feather in its beak, looked me straight in the eye and affirmed in her own special way that it is time, indeed, for Helen Jane and me to create our nest together.

Isn't life just funny that way?

Stage Two

Here I sit, weary and bleary-eyed, early on a misty Saturday morning some five days after we were supposed to close on our new home. "Supposed to" is the operative phrase here. Earlier on the day of what turned out to be a rescheduled closing, I had symbolically completed the transition from New Mexico to Arkansas by obtaining my Arkansas driver's license and car registration using our new address. I felt elated, almost giddy, to have made this commitment. That was how sure I was that this was a done deal—at least in my head I was sure.

Later that afternoon, after several false starts (in retrospect, a warning sign I, for one, had erroneously discounted), we had finally reached the signing table at closing. Very near the end of the process, our finance person left the room without fanfare, and a bit later our real estate agent apparently also had departed. I hadn't noticed. The sellers and Helen Jane and I were focused on matters of mutual interest and busy signing papers. I felt myself getting irritated at the owners over their unwillingness to let us have a brief, uninterrupted time with prospective contractors to obtain bids on contemplated work, and was moved to tell them so. It was an unfortunate move on my part in some ways, because I could feel people quickly becoming uneasy in my display. However, expressing my feelings did open the door for me to see why one of them had been so angry. "You don't like anything we have, not my red carpet, nothing!," she spewed. "And I'm not going to sit there and listen to you and contractors talk about how you're going to change everything!" Immediately I saw what lay beneath her seemingly unruly behavior: fear of rejection. The same feeling within myself that I had been unwilling to confront with total honesty when they had refused my request.

Finding myself immersed in this new understanding, in my heart I immediately forgave her past behavior in this regard and quickly back-peddled from my demands. Amidst my newfound compassion, I vowed in the sanctity of that pregnant pause to refrain from the possibility of hurting her feelings any further. I suddenly felt grateful for what, at first, had seemed like a blunder on my part. Interesting: by exposing my anger, it gave her permission to state what was at the root of hers and grace had fallen on the moment.

Momentarily, our finance person opened the door and beckoned for Helen Jane and me to join her. Puzzled, I excused myself, and as we entered the room I could see that our real estate agent was quite subdued. To make a very long story short, even after she had checked and double-checked the facts of the matter, while sitting in the closing our finance person had a sudden sense that something was wrong with our flood insurance document, so she called the insurance agent to see if what she feared was indeed true. What she found was that they had made a mistake in awarding us the insurance. In fact, they said, the community had once been associated with the federal flood insurance program (FEMA) but had, for some reason unknown to us, let the affiliation lapse, or so it seemed. In any event, because we could not get flood insurance in this flood plain location, the lender could not issue the mortgage.

The finance person immediately called the federal agency and found this information to be correct. The deal would have to be aborted. I could feel my stomach cramp, like someone was trying to wring the last bit of life out of my intestines. Despair overwhelmed me. I looked over at Helen Jane and she had turned pale white.

I recall wondering who would throw up on the other first. To say that we were flabbergasted at this news is a gigantic understatement, especially because this detail had been checked by both our finance person and real estate agent on numerous occasions. The pronouncement had taken the wind out of our sails and the fear of the unknown mushroomed like a fire doused with kerosene.

After all, we had moved all the way from New Mexico and now had our furniture in storage with a deadline to remove it just weeks away. I was growing tired of the tension and sheer exhaustion of it all. As if that weren't enough, we had invested whatever physical and emotional energy we had left obtaining costs and making selections pertinent to revamping the house into our home. Even so, it had suddenly become abundantly clear to both Helen Jane and me that the helicopter had saved us—and that we must not be so prideful as to deny that need. I shall explain.

Helen Jane and I have a distinct feeling that if something is "right" for someone, it, whatever it is, happens easily. Things and circumstances don't become burdens, but rather with ease, even expedition, they find their way to fulfillment. Yet, to our relative denial, all along the way we had an underlying feeling that blocks were put in the way. Everyone had just worked hard to eliminate them, that's all. The distinction here is not that they just vanished, easily, but that great effort had to be exerted to eliminate barriers to normal progress. We had let their eventual removal blind us to the fact that these were, instead of normal happenings, warnings of the inappropriateness of this purchase, despite the fact that on one occasion very near the end of the process we suggested to one another that all this was becoming just too difficult to be right. Only to deny this truth once again.

Of course, this is all in retrospect. We had committed fully to this purchase from the beginning, and when the final detail was exhaustively completed, the obtaining of flood assurance that guaranteed our mortgage from the lender, we went to the closing with great anticipation that in just a few days we would be able to begin our newest adventure. Then the seemingly disastrous news brought us to the sudden realization that we had been saved from ourselves. The meaning of a joke Helen Jane and I have found useful in such circumstances became our reality in the moment.

The story goes something like this. Once upon a time a man was watching television when the program was interrupted by a bulletin announcing a flash flood warning. "Ah," he dismissed, "not to worry, God will save me." Some time later, he heard a huge roar and again a warning came on the television, this time that the dam had burst and everyone was warned to evacuate immediately. "Ah," he dismissed again, " not to worry, God will save me." A few moments later, he looked out the window and saw the rushing water and a friend in a row boat beckoning him to get in. "Come on, John, get in. I'll save you from this," he hollered. "Naw," John responded, "not to worry, God will save me." A short time later, as he climbed to the second story for safety, John looked out the window to survey the situation and saw another friend in a motor boat. "Come on, John, I'll pull over there. Get in, I'll save you from this." "Naw," he responded again, "not to worry, God will save me." Not much later, when he was grasping the chimney to avoid being carried away in the flood waters, a helicopter came and dropped its rope ladder. A voice bellowed over the roar of the water and the torqueing blades of this iron bird, "Come on, mister, grab the ladder and we'll be able to save you from disaster." "Naw," he confidently dismissed one last time, "not to worry, God will save me." Well, needless to say, John drowned.

And when he went to Heaven, he was met by St. Peter, who greeted him lovingly. To which John responded, "St. Peter, I'm confused. I have terrific faith in God, yet he didn't save me from this disaster." "Didn't save you?!" St. Peter responded in disbelief. "For goodness sakes, John, first God sent you a row boat, then a speed boat, and finally a helicopter. How saved do you need to be?"

Yes, just like John, we had failed to see the row boat and the speed boat as life's offerings of safety. But the sudden, inner knowing that the helicopter had indeed arrived spoke to both Helen Jane and me simultaneously. Indeed, it had spoken to the depths of our being. So when our finance person announced to us that the deal was off, we instantaneously looked at one another and Helen Jane whispered, "Helicopter?" I confirmed the truth of that knowing with a simple nod. And a sudden, unexplainable, peace filled my heart—until fear reared its ugly head as the commanding force it is.

Even in a state of some newfound awareness I found myself confused, stunned and angry, and in short order I felt myself become despondent, even depressed. Who to blame? Who to fix it? Who to turn to? In a state of shock, we all went our ways, us to the bank to obtain a refund of our cashier's check, and then to the real estate office to sign the document which released us all from further obligation, so we could obtain our earnest money check. As I sloshed through the rest of the day, wading through the many murky questions that arose—with no apparent answers to any of them—I could only find solace in the inner sense that this was for the best, despite immense feelings of emotional woundedness. It even hurt to envision the pain the sellers must be in, after also moving to a new location in trusting anticipation. As I looked at Helen Jane, I couldn't help wonder if she felt as bad as I did. It didn't take a moment for me to discern that she did, maybe even worse.

I had an agonizing, fitful night. Helen Jane reported the same. Again, fear of the unknown tried to take control. How many times must we go through this? What's behind it all? What do we do now? The need to know overtook me for a time. Again, I prayed for inner peace and, after vowing to only watch the mind chatter instead of engaging it in battle, I finally lapsed into a stupor. When I awoke the next morning, I felt like I had been run over by a truck. Both my body and mind were that sore. And my emotions that raw.

During breakfast, we decided to drive over to our real estate agent's office to see if anything else had transpired, if anything had become clearer. Indeed it had. He greeted us by saying that the banker had just called to say that the property had been placed in the incorrect flood zone, which simply meant that even if the village was still associated with the government flood insurance program, we could obtain a maximum of only $35,000 insurance, which the lender obviously could not accept as a binder for our mortgage. The helicopter had done its deed. St. Peter had affirmed closure. The peace I had felt the day before now had meaning. And Helen Jane and I collapsed in an embrace.

At the very least, we learned that the seemingly good will show its face again and again, and the seemingly bad won't last forever. Life is ever-changing. Reality without denial. Comforting, isn't it?

So, now that the door to this episode has been closed, Helen Jane and I eagerly wait for the window to reveal our real home. Living in this Truth lets me know that this time it will be easy. Life sure is funny that way.

Stage Three

Helicopter, schmelicopter!! Isn't it interesting how we sometimes "manufacture" stories to fit the occasion in order to assuage our depression of the moment? Life sure is funny that way.

Life takes many turns, not literally one way then another the next, but circumstances and seeming "goods" and "bads" ebb and flow. It's only when we label and become attached to them that life becomes uncomfortable; first, when we label something as good and it turns out to be otherwise and then, when something appears to be bad and it isn't that at all. Only our fear out of proportion to the scene paints it that way. I guess the lesson is to refrain from labeling events and circumstances at all—and certainly—to refrain from attaching one's emotions to outcomes, real or imagined.

What has happened to us with the move to Arkansas and the seeming emotional roller-coaster we've been on regarding the purchase of our home could be seen in a much larger light—providing we were anything but human. You already know the first part. The rest goes something like this story that may be familiar to you. It seems like a wild horse found its way into a man's stable. A neighbor saw it and said to the new owner, "What good news. Now your son can learn to ride." "Ah," the man said, "good news, bad news, who knows?" Weeks later, while riding the horse the son fell off and broke his leg. The same man said to the owner, "Too bad your son broke his leg. What bad news." "Ah," the man said again, "good news, bad news, who knows?" As the boy was recuperating the army came marching through town looking for able recruits, and because of his broken leg, the young boy was spared. The neighbor commented yet one more time to the owner, "What good news. Had your son not broken his leg, he'd have to be in the army." "Ah," said the owner, "Good news, bad news, who knows?"

Our home-finding story seems to be going just that way. Good news, bad news, who knows?

Well, after determining that we'd been saved, a number of friends, even mere acquaintances, declared our "misfortune" good news: that we'd been saved from some disaster, or saved for something even better for us. Buoyed by these affirmations of what we just knew was our "good fortune," we were about to look for our "real" home, when the roof seemingly caved in yet again. One day we heard from our banker that she would be visiting with the government representative who deals with land/flood determinations, and that what he told her could change the conditions of the loan agreement for the previous contract. Needless to say, that put us on pins and needles through the weekend, as we awaited her call.

Late Monday afternoon we heard from her that yet another determination had been made regarding the location of the property on which we had made an offer. As bazaar as it may sound, the town of Beaver seemed to be in a flood zone, and was indeed affiliated with the proper flood agency program (FEMA), *but,* Beaver had not been mapped, so with only a "yes" or "no" option on the form to indicate whether Beaver was in a flood plain, without a definitive map to determine the correct answer, the government could not answer "yes," so they had to say "no." Can you imagine?! Regardless, with the determination indicating that the property was not in a flood zone, flood insurance was not necessary in order to acquire the mortgage. Now what to do?

By this time, we had so convinced ourselves that we had made the original offer by mistake and had been saved from it, our emotional energy was all tied up in that short-lived myth. By now it was mighty hard to turn the corner to recommit to the original decision. Until I received a perfectly-timed phone call from a wise and trusted friend late one night. "Jim, I received your note about your deal falling through. I've been praying on it for three days and just had to call you. What happened?" I explained, yet one more time, and offered the view that we felt we had been saved. "I would encourage you to think of this in another way," she rejoined. "I think what may have happened is the process and your thinking just got caught up in some negativity and, emotionally at least, you began to look for a way out of the deal. Rather than bailing out, I have a sense that this property is calling out for you and Helen Jane to bring it your deep love and creativity and to fill it with loving friends."

Her every word was clean and clear as a bell. She didn't need to say more. I knew instantly that she was right, as my inner tension from all this left me instantaneously and I was just as suddenly filled with deep, inner peace. I had, indeed, let myself be duped by self-deception, by not waiting for the large picture to show its head, that being the clearing up of the flood status for the town of Beaver. So our purchase would not now be clouded by an erroneous determination, which could cause conflict later on. Whew!

I shared this story with Helen Jane the next day, and she didn't quite buy it as a way for her to reconsider the matter. "I need some additional evidence," she proclaimed, and went about her way. The next day the evidence she needed showed up. z A letter from the sellers' lawyer laid out the terms of the original agreement, indicating that we were obligated to honor it now what the lending had been cleared up. An immediate conversation with our attorney determined, because the contract deadline had been exceeded long ago, that we would not have to honor it if we didn't want to. That made the field for making the decision clear, so Helen Jane and I discussed the purchase from the standpoint of the genuine affection we had for Beaver Town and the tremendous potential for the house to be our real home. The decision became simple, even easy, in these terms. In a moment's time we called our real estate agent and asked him to arrange the closing for the next afternoon.

That time has come and gone. And we are now the joyful owners of our new home in the town of Beaver, Arkansas. Good fortune, bad fortune, who knows? Life's just funny that way.

Stage Four

Thumpety, thumpety, thumpety, thump; thumpety, thumpety, thumpety, thump; thumpety, thumpety, CALAANGGG!; thumpety, thumpety..... So goes the (almost) rhythmic beat of vehicles crossing the last wood-plank expansion bridge in Arkansas, its ten-to-twelve foot timbers playing their tune like the vibrations of Lionel Hampton's xylophone. Well, almost like that. Except for the CALAANGGG, that is! The two expansion joints at both ends of the bridge offer a startling punctuation in the otherwise natural flow of life in Beaver Town, as we now call our new home. As Helen Jane puts it, if it weren't for the clang unnecessarily jolting our lives, living here would be almost ideal.

One would think that as we "ready ourselves for life in the new Millennium" (if I hear that phrase one more time, I'm going to re-label the years to avoid the crossover to the new era!), we could find enough intelligence to create a solution to the problem. Cover the expansion joins, or at least buffer them with a rubber compound, or some equivalent. Surely someone in this universe has the creative genius—or is it just plain common sense—to remedy the situation! Perhaps some folks are just too lazy or set in their ways to research it adequately and do the right thing. Or isn't it a real problem, after all? Is it just an excuse to keep from thoroughly enjoying a place called home? Or has it become the latest item to "victimize" the occupants of this tiny, quaint town?

Recently, when Helen Jane commented that the cars were waking her up in the early morning hours, requiring her to put in earplugs so she could sleep those last few minutes before waking for the day's events, I responded by saying, "No, the cars aren't waking you up, that's just being a victim. If it was the cars doing it, wouldn't I also be awakened by them?" A thoughtful, "Hmmmmmm," was Helen Jane's only response. "Perhaps it is that you won't let go of the world, even while you sleep," was my last comment, not wanting to push the discussion beyond just planting a seed for thought, something that might just provoke her to examine if she was contributing to the problem. Or maybe the annoying sound is just that. In any event, on every level of my being, I want *someone* to take responsibility for fixing it!

It's a shame that this irritant still injects itself into our lives, because nearly four months into our work on the property, the house is now beginning to show itself as a warm, comfortable, even inviting, home. A million dollar view: marvelous light casting its painterly-like imagery to and fro; an exquisite sunrise streaming through our bedroom French doors nearly every day; the comfort of breakfast in the loggia (a new term for us, meaning a lounge-like area, in this case, off the kitchen overlooking the flower- and tree-filled back yard); and so much more to be grateful for. Like having nice neighbors: friendly and helpful, yet respectful of our need for privacy. Yet we focus on the seemingly one thing that infests the soul, like a chigger just inside the waistband of one's underwear. The irritant serves as a constant reminder that all is not well, after all—even though life for the most part has become a paradise of sorts. Or is it instead a metaphor for the fact that life is just that way: filled with events and circumstances and beings that have no meaning at all, except the meaning we give to them? Each of us will have our own explanation for this, so it doesn't pay for me to project my own—beyond the obvious.

For example, here I sit, at my desk in the loggia, enveloped by an inspiration in the making. I hear the slight trickle of water from a miniature water fountain my brother and sister-in-law gave us last Christmas, its musical lilt embracing me much like the rich, sepia-toned photo of a gull soaring in the drafts of a Venice, California sunset, given to me by my youngest son, Todd, for Father's Day this year. A clay figure dramatically portraying a mother searching for her lost child on the Trail of Tears, sits on the top of my desk, reminding me of the compassion I try to keep foremost in my heart and mind; two photo transfer prints, one of a pair of horses dueling in a corral, the resulting dust playfully dancing in the Southwestern light and the other, a reflection in a mirror of some of the more important things in life, remind me, respectively, not to be afraid to express my life passionately and to take time to reflect deeply before making summations about circumstances and events and other beings. And to celebrate life and what I am and all others are, and to live non-judgmentally in the larger perspective life provides.

Buzzzz! I hear the interruption of the clothes dryer, seemingly for the third or fourth time, reminding me that Helen Jane is up in the guest house, painting and rearranging things. I feel a momentary irritation in the pit of my stomach, and quickly decide that the best way to fix it is not to ignore it, but rather to get up and empty the dryer of its contents without resentment. I am immediately rewarded for my decision to do the right thing. As I enter the kitchen, I am treated to the brilliant, early-morning sun streaming through the string of shutters that adorn the quintet of windows in the dining room, softly brushing a surreal light-and- shadow-filled painting across the mellow, heart-pine floor.

As I turn to pass through the living room, a brace of windows serve as picture frames, exhibiting the majestic view of the White River as it flows into Table Rock Lake. I begin to smile at the signs of true justice as I enter the master bedroom, the last bridge to the utility room in the master bath area, and am greeted by the sweet smells that only the start of a day in Beaver Town can produce. And there I was, just moments ago, superficially contemplating, perhaps even momentarily resenting, a fictional irritant in this moment's chapter of my life. My minds eye returns to the photograph of the reflective mirror, and my gut softens in gratitude.

I return to my laptop, sinking once again into that comfortable, inspiring space, and my attention is drawn affectionately to Helen Jane running the vacuum cleaner, probably finishing one room before she begins on the next. She's done such a wonderful job on all she's touched in this new environment. From first building her vegetable garden, to putting a superb finish on our new, raw, ash-wood kitchen cupboards, to laying tile in the utility room and building the rest of the railing on the front deck. And now she insists on completing the guest house by herself, a testimony, perhaps unwittingly, to wanting what will be her very own art studio for weaving, painting and writing, and the guest quarters, adorned in a Southwest motif, to be just like she is: filled with joy and welcome, like a warm embrace to a longtime friend. She certainly has invested her physical and emotional energy in these changes and I can see that she is (justifiably) proud of her life's work. It has not been easy for her to see herself in this light, and it warms my heart to see her now acknowledging the expression of her gifts this way.

On one hand, I could feel guilty that she's up there working herself to near exhaustion—and loving most of it to boot—and here I am, "just exercising my fingers on the keyboard." But we decided long ago to support one another in what one or the other thinks is important to do at the moment, usually after we've talked about it a bit. My previous way of dealing with her working and me not, would have been to manufacture something to do of at least equal value. The American way, I am afraid. Guilt and shame have a way of repeating themselves, like the little belches that emit after eating too many cucumbers.

I heard myself almost doing it again this very morning, mentally lining up some yard work to fill my day. Instead, I listened to an inner prompting and merely announced after breakfast that I had decided to write some today. Helen Jane responded to my decision with a joy-filled, "Oh, goooood! I hope you have FUN!" With that kind of support, how could I go wrong? She cheerfully bounced up the stone steps to the soon-to-be-art studio, and I instinctually declared that this is the way to live!

We have been blessed many times along the trail of our latest transition. What may have seemed like a catastrophe of the moment has usually turned out to be a miracle, or at least something for the long-term good of the house, and therefore us. In each instance, we found a new someone who lent a helping hand, sent us in a better direction, or advised us on a new way to look at something. A skilled, dependable carpenter for $15 an hour finds his way to our doorstep and shows us the more pragmatic, simple, ways of dealing with what we think are burning issues; a talented neighbor who completed a score or more of small projects merely for a trade of our old stove; two inexplicable, plugged toilets which led us to a plumber who worked late on a Friday night and early one Sunday morning to fix what could have been a major sewer replacement quite simply—and much less expensively; a corps of men, all over 60 who, as part of their church mission, moved our belongings from storage at no cost, and provided a bevy of incidents to keep us lighthearted along the way. My goodness—how blessed we were!

Just yesterday, while we were sitting in our living

room with two new friends—a husband and wife who run a nursery nearby, and who had volunteered to assist us in planning the kind of yard we want—Debbie, our neighbor, came to our back door with goodies in hand, as a celebration of our just moving into the main house. A cache of warm sweet rolls and dinner buns, the aroma just bursting into our nostrils and filling our lungs, affirmed the fact that she is, as her husband is not bashful to proclaim far and wide, the best baker in town. Once again we feel glad we're where we are. And just this morning, when I saw her husband leaving for work, I told him how good the rolls were, saying that there we sat, eating all that sugar, meaning how GOOD it tasted, when he interrupted me, saying, "Aw, don't let that be a problem. Just enjoy them." A cleaner, more wholesome, perspective once again. No guilt, no same. Just a moment to be savored.

The phone rings, and a female voice asks for me. It's the woman who manages the appliance store where we bought our new refrigerator.

"Remember our conversation about Amana rarely giving rebates?" she inquires.

"Yes," I say, "I remember it well."

After all, I always at least initiate a conversation of that kind when purchasing something, hoping for a discount of some kind. I justify my behavior, at least internally, by telling myself that that's just how one is supposed to behave when on a fixed income.

Anyhow, she says that she had just had received word of a rebate and we qualified for it, so to expect a check for $70 in the next six to eight weeks. What a delightful surprise! But more important than the money is the fact that she remembered us and did the right thing about it. Isn't life funny that way? Just when we debate the rightness of something or living somewhere, someone does just the appropriate thing to put things in perspective. I am *so* glad we live here! I believe deep in her heart, so is Helen Jane.

And deep in my own heart I feel certain that one of these days—I sense quite soon now—the CALAANGGG will suddenly disappear and the rhythm of Beaver Town will be without equal.

Finis.

Or not?

Stage Five

As I sit here typing this, I realize how much I miss the bridge, at least its more natural rhythms. It's been better than two years since I last reported on our local scene in Beaver and much has transpired.

Helen Jane and I have divorced, for one. How did it happen? Although I know I certainly contributed to our demise, I also know I'll never find out what really happened. It's difficult enough to know my own mind on such a heavy topic, let alone understand what's inside someone else's head or heart.

In the final analysis, I suppose it's good enough to know that I did my very best over a very long time to make it work. Part of "the all-American boy does his best no matter what syndrome," I guess. I suppose we both did our best under the circumstances. It's done and over with now, and I remain grateful for the gift of our relationship and the growth that came from it—from both its best moments and its worst. I'm a better person for having actively participated.

Not only that, but some new, refreshing "life's funny that way" stories have come of such goings on. One relates to the aftermath of my separation from Helen Jane. You'll recall that Helen Jane and I invested a great deal of time, energy and money in remodeling our home. When she decided to move out, the task of selling it was left to me. There I sat, with a house half-empty and in a temporary interior landscape that could only be viewed as a distress sale. So I maxed out my credit card and purchased enough furniture and appliances and such to return it to a homey atmosphere. It surprised me that doing so even to this degree, that is, reinvesting my energy in it, would make me fall in love with the space all over again; a real plus over the short haul. I was thoroughly enjoying the full comforts of home once again.

After a few false starts with potential buyers, one day seemingly out of nowhere a couple came to the back door unannounced, rang the cowbell adorning the back door and asked if they might see the house. Of course I welcomed them and showed them around. (Good thing I had given it a kiss and a promise cleaning earlier that day!) They asked the usual questions, and on the way out the door the gentleman of the family said what seemed like music to my ears, "You'll be getting an offer from us tomorrow." I'd heard such language before, never to hear from folks again, but this one seemed genuine.

Sure enough, I got a call the next morning and he asked if they could see it again that day, this time with his mother in law, who would be joining them in the purchase. My heart began to pound in anticipation. We made arrangements and upon arrival the husband asked if he could photograph the rooms, behaving like someone who had just purchased a home and wanted to send his friends and family pictures of it. Mother in law made her own inspection while the Mrs. sat with me on the living room couch, which made for a gorgeous panoramic view of the brilliantly lit hillside across the river.

During a lull in the conversation she perched this question in my mind: "Would you also consider selling all your furniture, everything but your personal belongings, in this transaction?" I must have made what seemed like a strange face to her. Actually it was only a startled look, but it evoked an apology from her, nevertheless. "No, no, your question is a legitimate one, all right, but it's just that no one has ever asked that of me and it's caused me to think without being ready to. To be perfectly honest, I'd be willing to consider your question, but feel we must keep it separate from the sale of the house, because I want to be absolutely ethical about the price of the house, so Helen Jane won't get the false impression that I've pawned one off against the other for my personal benefit." "I fully understand," she rejoined and we left it at that for the time being.

They all joined me in the living room and asked what we wanted for the house and I responded with the offer Helen Jane and I had agreed on. They thought if over a bit and said I'd hear from them later that day. As usual, they were true to their word and called with an offer, which, after some negotiation, we accepted. After the agreement was signed they re-approached me about the contents. "What do you actually mean by wanting all the contents?" I prodded. "Well, everything but your personal goods. We'd like all the kitchenware, all the furniture, carpets, TV, everything." "Not my art, though ?" "We'd consider that part of your personal goods," she said, but I would like to negotiate to purchase a number of your photographs."

Over the next few days we prepared our separate lists and agreed on a sale price. "What had I done?" was all I could think after signing that second agreement. Yet, in a flash, I realized that what I had done, in one fell swoop, was to rid myself of my past: all the belongings that could keep me trapped in the memories of a now defunct relationship and thus slow down my grieving process. Life sure is funny that way, not only to the degree that I was freed from an extraordinary emotional and spiritual burden, but also freed to do anything I wanted with my life without material encumbrance. Plus I would be able to pay off my credit card debt in full.

To make matters even more dramatic, during the time these folks were contemplating their offer, just hours, actually, out of the blue, or so it seemed at the moment, our town attorney came over to visit. It was highly unlike him to come over without calling first. He simply appeared at the front door and asked if he might speak to me about something that could be very important to my future. "I've got a deal for you that you can't refuse," was his opening line. In retrospect, I can just see the Universe saying, "Okay, Bill, enter the scene and make your pitch. Jim needs this—and now, not later."

We joined in the living room over coffee and he proceeded to explain that he and his wife had just successfully convinced his mother to move in with them across the street, thus making her small, but sweet, comfortable home available for rent. He went on to describe it to me: two bedrooms, two baths, a dining room-living room combination, sky lights, cozy kitchen and pantry and a car port. All at a monthly rent that was highly negotiable. He stressed that last point over and over again. I had to admit, he had my attention.

Without knowing what the status of my negotiations regarding the sale of the house were, he added, "Oh," I forgot to mention that it's fully furnished, with everything you could want, including furniture, sheets and towels—everything—dishes, silverware, you name it. And you can sort it all out to have any configuration you want." I gasped at the truth that there surely must be guardian angels in charge of my life.

He clinched it, as though he hadn't already, by saying that he and others around town had been looking for a place for me to live because they wanted me to stay, especially as mayor (he probably didn't want to be stuck being mayor, I told myself in a moment of self-doubt). He had me, just like that. "Come on over and see it with me now, and you can make up your own mind about it."

Well, you would now guess that I did, as well as knowing the negotiations went extremely well, leaving me with a monthly rent, including utilities and cable television for exactly what I could afford given my circumstances. And you think life isn't funny that way? If I wasn't convinced before, I sure am now!

At the time I first wrote this, I was still living in Beaver, in that very same warm, welcoming space. Actually it's also as mayor now—a long, but fun story to tell—but I'll spare most of the details. They can be found in another short story in this collection. The short version, however, is that I had become involved in various town activities, like being on the Zoning and Planning Commission and then being its chair, and then being asked to fill a vacancy on the City Council. Then, one fateful evening, everyone else beat me to the punch by denying their rightful opportunity to complete an unfulfilled term of our recently resigned mayor, and lo and behold, I was it. And now, I'm simply having a ball with it, and as long as I am, I'll stick with it. That, or until I feel it's time to move on—or the community feels its time I do. Either way, I feel blessed to have had the opportunity to serve this community, to be able to give what I have to it, and receive much more from the quality of life and relationships than I had ever anticipated.

One of the things I'm most pleased about is the reconfiguration of our bridge, the good ole' Golden Gate South. Nearly two years ago now, I called one of the chief state engineers to inform him that the wooden planks were in general disarray and needed a major overhaul. "Jim, your timing is impeccable. I've just been up that way with my wife," he confessed, "and have here on my desk a memo to another section of the department to see if we can't get every stick of wood on the bridge replaced, plus take care of those CLANGS on either end of the bridge."

An inner smile came crashing through at the synchronicity of it all, wondering how Helen Jane would have taken this news. I didn't have to fight him on a single thing as we pursued our conversation on the matter at hand. As a matter of fact, we agreed on every issue but one—well, at least initially. When I asked if he would also consider repainting it, he expressed great reluctance, mostly because of the cost. I just asked if he'd consider it and see what the real potential was. He allowed that consideration and we parted for the time being.

About a month and a half later, I called to see what was transpiring and our patron saint of bridges old and decrepit said that their was perfect agreement on the need to repair the bridge as suggested and the engineering design was already in the works. The painting? Well, perhaps his own crew could do it, he's have to look into it further. I won't drag this out, but in a few months he called me to say that indeed his crew could paint it and they were scheduled to begin the project just after the holidays.

Our patron indicated that they would paint the bridge silver to afford the best protection for rust, etc. I suggested that it would take more paint to do so using a silver color, because it would never cover the rusty gold paint currently on it in just one coat. "What color do you want it?" he prodded. "Gold." "Gold? You've got to be kidding." "No, I'm not kidding, that's the color it now is, and besides, the bridge is called Golden

Gate South and one of our streets is of the same name, so if you change the color, it causes some problems for us I'd rather not have." After a long pause, he rejoined with a promise that he'd look into it. Just a week later he called to say he had found an array of possible colors in a paint that would afford the same protective quality as the silver and would send up a color chart for me to choose from. He was true to his word and with the thoughtful assistance of several of the district highway folks we matched the chip to the only place on the underbelly of the bridge that hadn't been too badly faded by age and weather.

The long and short of it is that at this point in time every last stick of wood has been replaced and the bridge glows a bright gold once again. Our gal is all gussied up for the nostalgia ball! They did a grand job with it all, reconstructing it with a design that is stronger and even longer lasting than the last time they did it, over a quarter a century ago now.

At the end, the community had an appreciation lunch for the men who worked on the project. Folks chipped in with all kinds of dinner food and luscious desserts. The fellas filled themselves to the brim and we sent them back to work with boxes of mid-afternoon snacks, as though they hadn't eaten in weeks. We prepared certificates of appreciation for each person and a plaque for our patron saint, and a great deal of fun was had by one and all. The crowning event was the distribution of Beaver license plates, so the fellas could adorn either their trucks or favorite wall at home. They'd never been so honored, or so they said, and it was a touching event for us all. They went off to finish the job in the next few days, when a few of us gathered to bid our final farewells, with mixed emotions, to be sure.

The ole' gal just isn't the same though. No more thumpety thump thumps. No more clangs. Just a slight rumble and still about the same amount of speeding over it beyond the limits—weight-wise, too—both despite the new stop signs on either side of the bridge and new weight-bearing warnings. She sure is pretty, though. Especially in the early morning sun, as it pierces the fog that skims the river beneath its bows, and then again in the late afternoon reddish cast that replicates the glow of San Francisco's own Golden Gate Bridge.

It matches the glow I get down deep inside every time I see someone stop alongside, pausing to photograph it for posterity. One thing for sure: she's etched an extraordinary image on the lining of my heart forever.

In the shadow of all this I was inspired to write a piece of poetic verse about all this and it follows. Does this end my stories about all this? I doubt it, but it does for now. Is any of this simply good news or bad news? Who knows for sure? All I know at this point is that life sure is funny that way. The gifts just keep unfolding, even if

sometimes they don't look like gifts when we
first see them. Appearances, and the assumptions
that accompany them, are just like that: hardly
ever the real thing. I guess it's not our job to
judge, only to wait patiently for the discernment
that will surely follow.

In any event, here's the piece de resistance:

"DANCING WITH AUNT NOSTALGIA

most of us have a favorite aunt
whose eccentricities
or strength of character
take us time and again
into the memories called nostalgia

our Beaver bridge is like that
filled with its own brand of charm
the golden rainbow expanse
glimmering in the late afternoon sun
the thumpety thump thump
ka-lang
thumpety thump thump
thumpety thump thump
ka-lang
announcing its belonging to the rhythms of
nature

carrying us across its breathtaking view of the
River White

but now she's getting a facelift
with 179 lb. replacement floorboards
interlaced as a sturdy affront to vehicles large and
small
that'll dutifully wear her down over the years
yet now noiseless in its affect.
no more thumpety thump thumps or ka-langs
to bump us in the night
with stop signs on either end to slow the
oncoming traffic
and avoid mid-bridge confrontations
(what fun those were to watch!)
and a new coat of makeup
brightly golden once again
all gussied up for the dance
of another twenty something years

it could take some doing
in this oncoming era of quiet transformation
to project the feeling of homey belonging once
again
or we could choose instead
to see it as but another life our favorite aunt's
been given
to bring yet another generation along

to the heartwarming dance of nostalgia
called Beaver."

Finis--For Sure! Or so I thought.

It's now several years later, and I have moved to Oregon. I still wonder as I reread this poem how this refurbished old dame would have found herself in Helen Jane's view. I hear she's extremely happy now in her own farmhouse south of Fayetteville. Yet another childhood dream of hers fulfilled, I realize in the wake of it all. My heart warms in appreciation of all she is, and for this genuine happiness in her life. Good for her—good for me—good for us—I hear myself proclaiming inwardly on this beautifully sunlit, richly textured, autumn day.

Who knows what will come this way next? The only thing I really know for sure is that it won't be good news or bad news, either one. It'll only be funny in its very own way.

And don't I just *love* that by now?

ON PIGEONS AND OTHER IMPORTANT MATTERS

I want to tell you about making love. Not about simply f---ing, but, really, about making love. There is a difference. A really big difference. Or at least that can be so.

I've written other things about making love, like over 350 poetic verses all starting with: MAKING LOVE IS. They're about the kind of loving that exudes from character in every instance one finds him or her self completely aware of current place and circumstance, totally present in the oneness that life simply and beautifully is. Whenever I'm asked what I do for a living, I'm so taken by this truth that I often answer, "Oh, I just make love all day." But that is not today's story.

Actually, I came to the computer this morning prompted by an extraordinarily enjoyable and fulfilling reading of Anne Lamott's rendering on writing and living, *BIRD BY BIRD*. No matter how I was moved or tickled, and there was a great deal of both as I invested in soul nourishment in the wee hours of this morning and the last, my mind kept taking me back to a treasure of a story she shared about her son, Sam. It goes like this:

"My son, Sam, at three and a half, had these keys to a set of plastic handcuffs, and one morning he intentionally locked himself out of the house. I was sitting on the couch reading the newspaper and I heard him stick the plastic keys into the doorknob and try to open the door.

"Then I heard him say, 'Oh, shit.' My whole face widened, like the guy in Edvard Munch's *Scream*. After a moment, I got up and opened the front door.

' 'Honey,' I said, 'what'd you just say?'

'I said, "Oh, shit," he said'
'
'But honey, that's a naughty word. *Both* of us have absolutely got to stop using it. Okay?'

He hung his head for a moment, nodded, and said, 'Okay Mom.' Then he leaned forward and asked confidentially, 'But can I tell you why I said "shit?"'

'Sure, honey, why?"

'Well, I said oh shit because the fucking keys don't work.'

Fantasy keys won't get you in...."

I find the story delightful, and it was the last line quoted that touched a space within me that made me realize that much of what we know and do about loving is based on fantasy. It was an inferential leap that got me here, but having made that leap in faith, I was propelled into the understanding that we are governed by all kinds of fantasies that keep us from loving as we were created to be.

It's fantasy's keys that have messed up our lives—for fantasies open the doors only to illusions, not Truth. Illusions, and not Truth, thus come to govern our lives. Years ago Joni Mitchell wrote a haunting song about illusions: *Both Sides Now*. In it she speaks about how love's illusions and life's illusions seem to have kept her from living her truth. If one were to listen closely to not so guarded conversations at social events or even eavesdrop on conversations between friends, it would become abundantly clear, and profoundly sad, that sex, and/or making love, is filled with illusions. And we're all guilty of perpetrating and perpetuating them into eternity.

In the first place, love-making isn't simply about fornication. No matter how we say "it," "it" isn't simply just about procreation. Nor is it simply about the rush we get while serving our infatuation to the fullest, either. And it certainly isn't something only men like to do. It's something we all ARE. No, not f---ed up. Lovers. Each of us is created in the image and likeness of Love. Our innate way of Being, that knows nothing but Loving. For that is what Love simply, perfectly, and infinitely is. That being the case, then, our only real purpose in life, and the only thing, therefore, that will fulfill us, are acts of making Love. Or, if it makes you feel better, acts of creating Love.

My experience, particularly with those financially less fortunate, let us say, has been nothing but deep connectedness; a merging of souls at the most profound level. The resulting photographs have blessedly matched the sensitive exchange of loving energy that etches their images indelibly on the lining of my heart. It is with that anticipation that I traveled to San Miguel, and I was not disappointed.

I want to share a story about how I came to appreciate even more the difference between making love, in any reference you wish to make of it, and being loving. It's a story about two pigeons. "Pigeons?" you say. "You really have gone mad!" No, quite the contrary. I merely have been given the extraordinary opportunity to witness, in the most tender and innocent way, the act of being a lover, a *real* lover. In a real sense it is a story about Being Love through all, and it was shown to me stripped from the personal nature of my own life, so I could see it with a bit more objectivity than otherwise would be the case.

A few months ago I went on a photo trip to San Miguel de Allende, Mexico. I had longed for that trip for over a year, for I have often had the good fortune to collaborate with these marvelously open and celebratory Mexican people in creating some stunning photographic imagery.

One day, as I approached the end of this awe-inspiring photographic adventure, I was moved to give myself a treat at a special place for lunch. Contrary to the ecstasy I felt during the overwhelmingly majority of the collaborative ventures with my camera in hand, I was feeling low after having just photographed a lovely teenage school girl, a portrait of seeming innocence, who immediately flung out her open palm on the end of her arm like a giant bullfrog's tongue snapping out to catch a passing fly, expecting me to pay her.

As fate would have it, deep in this self-created malaise, I looked up to get my bearings and found myself right in front of the restaurant I had in mind: La Capilla, the chapel. As I passed from the well-swept cobblestone street through the finely chiseled stone entry, I was overwhelmed at the sight: a two story winding staircase, elegantly fastened to the side of the largest cathedral in town, intertwined with the greenest ivy I've ever seen. The stone walls were fashioned in the same manner as the entry, and made for a startling demonstration of strength and power. Love seemed to be everywhere present.

As I headed toward the stairs, I noticed the large room off to the right, adorned in row after row, basket after basket, of festively wrapped goodies: biscochitos, jams and jellies, and fancy chocolates, each a necessary evil for those who occasioned La Capilla. I arranged to purchase several jars of exotic homemade jam: strawberry-basil, pineapple-raspberry, blueberry and peach, pear and cranberry, and another I can't recall, as it has long since passed through my digestive system. Must be a Pisces thing: I can't buy just one jar of jam or only one plant to save my life. I arranged to have these treats wrapped for travel while I had lunch, and the young, dark eyed woman with an infectious smile began the task immediately.

I was so taken by the contrast of this image with my most recent photographic encounter that I asked if I might create the young lady's photo. Long ago I began a series of this kind, using the inexpensive throw away cameras to photograph people with whom I felt some special bond. She quickly agreed, and I created our picture, beckoning her close enough so I could get both of us in the frame within an arm's length; hence the name of the series: *Within An Arm's Length.*

Immediately I began to feel my energy shift with this newfound imagery feeding my soul, and was completely uplifted by the time I climbed the winding staircase to bask in the view of the Jardin nestled in the surrounding architecture and landscape, embraced by the sound of tinkling wind chimes and babbling waterfall. A brilliant blue sky filled with billowy white clouds completed the picture of Heaven on Earth: a perfect setting for lunching on life's real gifts.

It was about 1:30 PM and yet I was the only one there to enjoy this luxury. It perplexed me for a moment, until I asked the waiter if lunch was indeed being served. He caught my ignorance in the matter and simply indicated that it would be awhile before others would be joining me. He was absolutely correct; the waiter and I shared this time and space for more than an hour with no one but each other. After ordering a quail salad, a continental style fish dish, and a glass of sauvignon blanc, I settled in to read a book by Joel Goldsmith, a metaphysician and spiritual writer who extends Mary Baker Eddy's Christian Science healing beyond that norm by some distance.

As I turned the pages to my bookmark, I heard an inner prompting to look over my left shoulder to the stone ledge that separated the two-story,

Spanish-tiled roof line from the furniture-filled rooms in the antique store below. Just as I looked over, two pigeons landed and strutted along the ledge past one another, not particularly paying attention to each other. I watched for a moment and noticed that one was beginning to approach the other, and I intuitively knew I was about to witness "the act." Seemingly without notice, one bird leaped onto the backside of the other, did his thing in a flash, and leapt back off to the ledge. In a few seconds, he repeated "the act" in precisely the same fashion. I was tickled by this version of modern man and woman in an after the marriage clinch. "Slam, bang, thank you, Mam," as the all too familiar chauvinistic expression goes. Just like that: land, do it, it's done and over with.

After privately thanking these lovely creatures for allowing me to participate vicariously in their clinches, I returned to my book and chilled glass of wine, dripping with dew cast by the now warm, humid day on the ice-cold goblet. Neither my reading nor wine sipping lasted very long, however. Just as I had been prompted the last time, I found myself returning to what I had decided was to be some kind of lesson for me. For nearly 45 minutes these two beautiful creatures billed and cooed, strutted around and brushed against one another, poked here and there, gently nudging under the wings, around the neck, beak to beak. It was the most extraordinary display of "after play" I have ever witnessed, despite my own preference for similar comforting under such conditions.

I notice that a few other diners had entered and they seem to glow in the wake of the beauty I had witnessed. As I prepare to leave, a man and woman at the next table catch my eye and we exchange a brief greeting.

I am walking on a cloud and want to share this story with anyone who would listen, but decide to savor the occasion privately instead, filling my soul to overflowing with joy.

The purpose of all this? Well, it could be to illustrate that making love isn't simply f---ing at all, although making love certainly could include that. Making love is really about what happens around the f---ing.

On another level, this marvelous display of being lovers depicted what loving is all about, while at the same time putting the sex act into a wholesome perspective. Sex is but a natural act between lovers, an act not unlike pecking at food, flying from one ledge to another, like dropping a load of feces on someone's Easter bonnet in the bowels of the Jardin below. But it also is a necessary act, one that comes with simply being an animal or spiritual being, either one. It is not something to withhold or talk down about. It simply is—like life itself. And when we make nothing more of it than that, it flourishes as a normal, even enjoyable, part of living.

When embraced as a wonderful gift of love, and created in the true sense of collaboration—fully giving and fully receiving—where two people give all they have to it, letting all expectations and restraints flee out of the relational window, making love in the larger sense becomes a sacred act, one that fulfills on the deepest level. Under these conditions, even the simplest form of love making transforms into Eros, our ultimate example of Oneness between two lovers.
In this context, the sex act itself becomes simply one more sacred demonstration of making love, of being a lover: just like making dinner for another, or picking up the other's laundry at the dry cleaners, hugging at the ankles and knees at bedtime, or catching one another's loving glance when passing the raspberry jam over brunch in front of a glowing fire on a frosty weekend morning. It is Eros in the human heart that transforms f---ing into F--ing; transforming momentary vulgarity into the sacred act of making or creating Love, moment-by-moment, day-by-day.

The billing and cooing? That is the story of stroking one another throughout life's moments, of caring enough about another to invest one's unbridled love with him or her. It is lavishing love on another for their benefit, because it's important to be lavished upon, at the very least because it says one is worthy of such treatment. But such treatment also rewards, in fact, greatly nourishes, the giver as well. For when we are allowed, privileged—whatever—to give love in such dimensions, especially when we are allowed to lavish love on another, we are fulfilled in a most profound manner. As we come to Love in such lavishness we become supreme Lovers in our own right.

This is what it means to be a Lover, a Lover of the first order—making Love all day long. It's no wonder that most want this job! We are made in Love's image so we, too, can experience Eros in its deepest meaning. So we, too, can lavish and be lavished upon. So we could, at last, be Lovers of the first order, without limitation.

When we are, we, and thus our lives, become nothing but Eros. If only we would get out of our own way and stop taking ourselves so seriously.

And forget most everything anyone ever taught us about making Love.

SURRENDER

The term "surrender" is often taken to mean a capitulation to some outer influence, a caving in or acquiescence rendered out of fear or a sense of powerlessness. As a basis for this rendering, however, surrender takes on a deeper, spiritual meaning.

Surrender speaks to a letting go of ego consciousness and self-importance, and instead aligning our presence with the full awareness of inner wisdom—that still, small voice that surpasses all intellectual and emotional understanding.

This noble act is one of true humility, where conventional authority is abandoned for a deeper source— and where our spiritual character and true identity are found. Naked, we stand before that inner voice, the tongue that speaks spiritual Truth, in full acknowledgment of its power in our lives. When fully aware, we surrender completely and thus activate our innate spiritual communion with endless gifts of healing grace.

The journey that brought the following images to thefore began more than a decade ago, during a conversation with an artist friend, Louise Roach, in Santa Fe, New Mexico. I wanted to create a single image depicting how marginalized groups and persons are often persecuted, and yet, even when crucified, nevertheless, show great compassion and empathy for others. It quickly became apparent that both the idea and process were unworkable at the time. Louise suggested I meet with an extraordinary artist in her own right, Patti Levey, her friend. I sensed a pathway had been opened for a new consideration.

Indeed, it was. During breakfast one morning, Patti volunteered to be a model and suggested that we gain permission to use an abandoned church in Alcalde, New Mexico, to initiate the project. With no more than a vague idea and a spirit of openness that paved the way for a choreography based on spontaneity and mutual trust, Patti and I linked in a spiritual dance that allowed freedom of expression to prevail.

We were greeted at the front door by a playful, curious dog and a weathered cross, the latter buried in scatterings of wilted wild flowers and dried weeds that had once served another purpose. After brief discussion, I lifted the cross onto Patti's shoulder, and we entered the inner chambers of the church. It became immediately obvious that the sacred chambers we then entered represented our own spiritual cathedral, from which flowed the inspirational guidance that graced this collection of images. The shadowed light was enchantingly compulsive to our purpose. After several such sessions, Patti suggested that we invite a model friend of hers to participate. Daniel Sogan did indeed join us, adding a commanding presence and a perfect complement to the collaboration. Although Daniel has since passed, his stunning images, not unlike Patti's, provided living testimony to the gifts of Life.

It soon became clear to me that the imagery spoke to various ways in which nakedness, crucifixion and surrender have been conveyed over the centuries, and how those terms also serve as metaphors for how we could not only learn to engage suffering in our lives, while also learn to keep from letting it cripple us from day to day. I began to feel a rich, spiritual texture unfold as we let light find its way into darkness, exposing the demonstration of inner reality onto the outer world.

I came to see the human form as an extraordinarily beautiful vessel for conveying life as a series of metaphors whose purpose to reflect deeper, spiritual meaning—images of spiritual

Truth that await only a fresh, virgin-like perspective. I recognized that this was not a commonly held view, yet it is one that speaks to me, both from the images that found their way onto film, and from the spontaneity of the collaborative process itself. I encourage you to take meaning from your own inward Source.

One viewer, for example, has suggested that these images could well speak to the Scriptural relationship between the Master Jesus and Mary Magdalene. Given the context of spiritual expression, they could provide visual testimony to the compassion and personal agony Mary Magdalene must have felt as she accompanied Jesus on his thorny quest to spiritual resurrection and transcendence.

Because of the nature of committed relationship, what another goes through often feels as though we are undergoing it along with them. Such powerful relational attachment is sure to crucify when we attach our life story to that of another. And we thus are not being true to ourselves, but rather to the effects of attachment. Through such pain we come to comprehend that attachment, too, must be surrendered if we are to be resurrected to a new—spiritual—way of life.

In my own case, I came to comprehend the imagery as an array of metaphors that emanate froma daring embrace with vulnerability: "standing naked before God," before the Truth of our existence. Thus, although nakedness is physical, it also speaks spiritually, as a metaphor. The spiritual context allows us to redefine nakedness to mean that our minds and emotions can be cleared— made naked, laid bare— shedding the threadbare clothes of old beliefs, feelings, and opinions in favor of inner wisdom, Truth. When we surrender these ego conscious remnants we return to the innocence from which Truth speaks. Henceforth, we awaken each day with infinite opportunities to live afresh.

Given this context of innocence, the images in

this collection can speak to a wide range of expressions that reflect our profound inner connection with spiritual Truth, while at the same time engaging life's circumstances and situations. Some may well speak to the burdens various cultures place on women—and the necessity to surrender those burdens, both on the part of women as well as those who so forcefully and unjustly render them—so that sovereign freedom for women and from the guilt associated with unfounded bias can at last reign.

The surrendering of burdens placed on men is no less important. Indeed, there are those impositions that would have men bury, rather than fully embrace, the more feminine aspects of intuition, receptivity, innocence, and the ability to nourish others—those very elements necessary to balance and complete us all. Likewise, women could be called to demonstrate so-called masculine character traits—like leadership and action-orientation—in order to create and maintaina balanced life within and without, rather than laying such responsibilities at the feet of their male counterparts or competing with them on their level.

The same principles found in spiritual Oneness can be applied to burdens placed on other disenfranchised groups and persons. None of us needs another to complete us or to compete with. Rather, our innate need is to celebrate life with those whom we can freely share our own spiritual completeness. The limitations of belief and opinion speak to the material plasticity in which we wrap our lives, the veils we hold dear, yet that keep us from looking within in order to one day to claim and demonstrate our spiritual perspectives.

After all, we do crucify others and ourselves, usually by distorting or failing to listen carefully to our inner Truth, in favor of acting out false assumptions about life in general, and personal relations in particular.

The feminine nature also speaks to the awareness

of the need to cut loose or surrender aspects of ourselves in order to make room for new beginnings. It is only by creating a space for the new that our personal resurrection can be made whole. Of greatest importance to me is that we learn to perceive life non-judgmentally—with each of life's circumstances and confrontations containing the opportunity for demonstrating the essence and embodiment of love. As we let ourselves see one another as reflections of our common divine essence, we come to treat both others and ourselves with the dignity spiritual essence commands of us.

Thus our only imperative is to listen while inner wisdom—inspiration/intuition—seeks our awareness. When regularly witnessed, we come to demonstrate only the sacred imprint with regularity. Such demonstration is like turning the kaleidoscope of life with just a slight twist, in order to obtain an entirely new, beautiful image—in this case, reframing the context from which to discern the journey less taken.

Finally, perhaps Hans Küng's comments can be helpful:

"There are many that hang on the cross: not only unsuccessful revolutionaries prisoners, those condemned to death; not only the incurably sick, the complete failures, those who are weary of life and those who despair of themselves and the world. There are many who hang on the cross: tormented by cares and oppressed by their fellow men, overwhelmed by demands and worn out by boredom, crushed by fear and poisoned by hatred, forgotten by friends...Is not everyone in fact hanging on his (or her) own cross?"

A more penetrating comprehension of Küng's contextual framework could indeed lessen the force of those thoughts that frighten us, lest we lapse into the cynicism and skepticism that are so plentiful in today's domesticated, often chaotic society.

In a spiritual sense, the cross represents our continual attention on life around us, an erroneous focus on outer appearance instead of inner awareness. By focusing on appearance, we obviate our inner knowing, gnosis—our inherent, eternal consciousness—thus nailing ourselves on the cross of illusion. Until and unless we focus inwardly to become One with the infinite consciousness that is our Being, we are crucifying ourselves moment by moment.

Yet, in a stroke of spiritual awareness, we

are resurrected into Being what we truly are: the undeniable conscious awareness of the ineffable One and only. Thus, for me, when photographing from our heart space— instead out of our need to

simply capture an image of outer appearance—the moment we reframe our lives out of the realization that in our innermost Being we are One, we are prompted to release the shutter, indelibly etching this image on our hearts as but another reminder.

Of this we can be sure: we already have all we

need for this spiritual journey. When consciously aware, each succeeding step will be birthed out of the womb of silence, through the voice of inspiration/intuition—the language Love, inner Wisdom, speaks.

Our only necessity is to stay fully aware, so the gifts of grace can infill and become our day-to-day reality. Indeed, through surrender come the emanations of innocence that transform. When embraced fully, we are resurrected and transcend into another world —from the world of a fear-filled mind to the world of the fearless, love-filled heart.

So ends the story of the creative dance. Happily so.

OTHER BOOKS BY JIM YOUNG

(See www.theinwardway.live for descriptions)

Swimming with the Mosquitoes

Defend as if True

Saving Grace

The Inward Way

Inside Silence

Ruminations; Conversations with Rumi

Insights

With Eyes to See

Imaginings

God's Pocket Dictionary; Newly Expanded

Sip and Savor

The Three Questions; A Simple Process for Spiritual Fulfillment

Perfect—Just Like You!

Aware in a World Asleep

The Invitation

Surrender (e-book only)

2013! The Beginning is Here

Priceless Pearls for Misguided Seekers

On Making Love; Spiritual Testimony to the Gift Life Is

As If From God

Letters Left Behind

God's Pocket Dictionary

What If...? Changing Your Life to Fit Your Truth

Living an Extraordinary Life in an Ordinary Reality

The Creation Spirit; Expressing Your Divinity in Everyday Life

A Labor of Love; Weaving Your Own Virgin Birth on the Loom of Life

Keys to the Door of Truth; The Metaphysical Musings of a Born-Yet-Again

Only Mind Matters; Emerging From the Waters of Symbolic Meaning

Defrocking the Gospel of Thomas

JIM YOUNG

Dr. Jim Young is an award-winning spiritual author, poet and program presenter. A practicing graduate of the Pecos Benedictine Monastery School for Spiritual Directors, Young is also President Emeritus of SUNY College at Potsdam, NY, Chancellor Emeritus of the University of Arkansas at Little Rock and former visiting Minister Emeritus of the Creative Life Church in Hot Springs, AR (New Thought). He is also co-founder of the Aristotle Group and the Arkansas Metaphysical Society.

A contributor on spiritually-oriented Internet programs, Young faithfully follows his inner calling by writing about and leading others from various religious and spiritual traditions to deeper, life-changing meaning and purpose for them.

Jim's writings, presentations and teachings re-frame Life's journey from one of separation and the chaos separation engenders, across the spiritual threshold to Oneness, and the inner joy and peace that witness this perspective.

Dr. Young is a gifted inspirational speaker who often uses Life's stories to convey spiritual meaning, and inspires others to look within for the Truth that transcends the superficial.

JIM YOUNG'S WEBSITE

www.theinwardway.live This website contains additional creations to come through Jim Young, including an introduction to a newly-produced Internet spiritually-oriented radio program, also by the same name.

Email: creationspirit@gmail.com

Made in the USA
Monee, IL
22 May 2021